*Present Yourself Powerfully
to Anyone, Anywhere*

FILMMAKER TURNED SPY TRAINER REVEALS:

WINNING
PRESENCE

FOR BUSINESS PRESENTERS

Produced and Distributed By
SagePresence LLC
(612) 384-0763
www.SagePresence.com

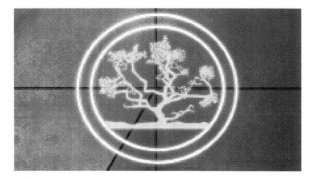

SagePresence
6201 134th Street West
St. Paul, MN 55124

ISBN: 978-1-6203023-2-3

Dedication

To the people who need a little help, a boost of confidence and the permission to hold their heads as high and stand as tall as possible. Sometimes doing what needs to be done means saying what needs to be said. Present yourselves to the world, and may the honor be mine in pointing you in the direction of the answers that lie within.

To the many people in business and filmmaking who helped me discover my own voice. And to Lauri Flaquer, who guided me to stay true to myself and shine as brightly as I can without holding back.

To my business partner, Pete Machalek, who brings the yang that balances my yin. The content of this book is the culmination of more than a decade of co-creation, application and perfecting of this material.

The journey hasn't been an easy one but traveling it together has always been exciting and meaningful. The words herein may be mine but the expression is ours together.

To my wife Kim, and my sons Ethan and Aaron, with love. We've all shared in the leading and the following in our family. We've learned to unmask our authentic selves and in the process are together discovering and creating who we are.

Table of Contents

Prologue

MINISTER: When you light a lamp
for someone else, you brighten
your own path too.
Script from the movie
"Transsiberian"

Some know me as a film director, others as the guy who taught acting to spies. Many experience me a speaker, or call on me when the stakes are high and they want to win.

I think of myself as a guy who lets little birdies out of cages. I set things free and protect the vulnerability around me. That's how I direct, speak, teach, coach, and win—by getting people to embrace and expand the part of them that's vulnerable—so they can get out of their cages of safety and fly like they were meant to.

Winning presence is about being confident enough to stop holding back. The largest advancements in influence are not the usual targets of continuous improvement that add experience, credentials and status to the armor you've been fortifying for years like a false front. Despite obvious advantages to appearing strong and impenetrable under pressure, the art of persuasion is more about releasing the part of you that has been hiding. What's in you that still gets scared and bruised is also the source of your passion and the key to winning presence— sharing bravely the very part of you that inspired protective measures in the first place.

We're all fragile inside, even the strongest among us, and our worry about that confines us. Nobody does it to us. We lock ourselves away inside cages of comfort. The bars of our cages are velvet lined, padded and soft, yet strong as iron to make us feel safe from the risks that accompany authentic expression.

You are constantly polishing the veneer and adding coats of lacquer, protecting the inside by emphasizing the outside. Meanwhile life passes you by, while part of your authentic self remains hidden underneath, unfulfilled and unexpressed.

Each coat of protection was added after an experience that made you feel vulnerable. You took a risk and got burned. You went out on a limb and it broke. You expressed yourself passionately but were misunderstood, or laughed at.

We portray ourselves to the world with our strengths forward and try to hold back everything that's sensitive or delicate. We present ourselves incompletely, restrained by our need to feel safe from the uncertainty of trying to influence someone else. We want to stand up for what we want, believe or perceive in our mind's eye, but we doubt ourselves; we fear failure and rejection. There's always someone else with better credentials, and more legitimacy, status, power or charisma than we think we have so our yang tries to protect our yin by hiding anything vulnerable. We force a calm though our heart is pounding, stifle our passion so we won't appear overeager and we smile over our pain so we don't look weak. Then, half-hidden inside our protective cage, we stand in our most important moment to speak flatly, incompletely and unfairly to ourselves, forever to wonder, "What if ?"

To be certain the vulnerable feeling won't come again, we stay in our cage.

Freeing the Powerful Presenter Within

I remember the day I freed myself to take command and share my authentic self under pressure. Despite perceived risks, I bravely revealed my passion. Instead of protecting my reputation, I *created* it.

My confidence was sourced in authenticity, not the false front image I previously relied on. I took ownership of the moment without holding back, becoming strong and vulnerable at the same time, on a level I couldn't put to words before writing this book.

I felt that the winning presence did its work almost invisibly. Like the covert agents I was training at the time, my influence was as much under the radar as it was overtly apparent. My words and content were clear and strong, but I was reaching them at deeper levels. I was operating behind enemy lines where no one was looking to be won over. They were focused on the overt—the exterior of my communication—,while I was inside them, dealing with their fears and dreams.

To have their hearts, I had to release the vulnerable part of my own heart under the kind of presenting pressure that would have held anyone back— anyone but me.

I freed myself from the protective shell at the peak of my instinct to hide. I was riding quietly in an armored car, in a compound called the Federal Law Enforcement Training Center (FLETC for short, pronounced "Flet-see"), somewhere in southern Georgia.

It had been the perfect entrepreneurial coup—filmmakers teaching acting to spies—but I was way out of my element and in unforgiving territory. In my past, I'd seen a chunk of the world and had run and sold two businesses. I directed an indie feature film that got a Warner Bros. release, put the first computer game in a cereal box and the first CD-ROM in *Rolling Stone* magazine. I had advertised movies like "Godzilla," "Jumanji," and "Die Hard III" on the Internet, and co-created the Energizer Bunny® screensaver. I'd directed a lot of performers but today I was afraid.

This was not fiction I would be directing. This was reality, where actual covert agents were going to bet their success and survival on their ability to pull off an acting role. Relying on what I would teach them, the audience these agents would eventually face would be real bad guys carrying guns with live bullets, and they'd be eager to spot a weak performance. It made me worry about my own performance—which would surely be under the harshest scrutiny I'd ever experienced.

I was having the distinct experience of being the farthest away from home I'd ever been.

At my side was my trusted collaborator Pete Machalek, looking particularly naïve for following me. I expressed my misgivings, and he retorted with credentials, a masters degree in film and communication and the logic that our knowledge of acting technique would apply quite directly to these spies.

I think he was giving me the same spiel I made up to sell the agent who hired us—just words to get a job. Pete looked like Mr. Spock to me, sitting there emotionless. I knew we were both aliens going where no one had gone before, and all the Vulcan logic of the Federation wasn't going to make me comfortable. This was a make-or-break moment, and I knew my worrying could affect my performance. I needed confidence but I had self-doubt.

I am normally quite emotionally intuitive. For as long as I can remember, people have come to me to talk about the emotional things they were struggling with, and in these conversations, the right thing to say—reassuring, supportive and useful—always popped into my head. But today the emotions were mine and they were drawing me back into the cage. I needed to take flight with everything I had to give.

The FLETC compound was of unknown acreage. We left the area with all the buildings and were winding along a stretch of road through a field, passing the occasional half-buried bunker with grass and weeds being invisible rooftops when seen from the air. Suddenly, our driver stopped.

> DRIVER: We have to wait for an all-clear from the off-road pursuit training unit.

Suddenly, two SUVs screamed out of a break in some trees, kicking up dust and brush as they launched across the road in front of us. Moments later, a VOICE crackled over the radio.

> DISPATCH: Transport five. You are clear to proceed to checkpoint one-bravo.

The armored vehicle proceeded into the woods, and I thought about how I'd gotten to such a strange place. When Pete initially approached me with the business idea of training professionals with acting, I resisted. But one day, the phone rang, and it was the Department of the Interior looking for filmmakers to train spies. I couldn't pass it up. Of course, the first thing I did when I got the call was hang up on them because the idea seemed so preposterous that I thought it must have been my brother Jon, making another of his infamous prank phone calls.

I took the gig for the story I would get to tell. A young Ronald Reagan had trained undercover agents, but as far as these agents knew, Dean Hyers and Pete Machalek would be the first *filmmakers* to try their hands at teaching in a school for spies. A story like that would leave my fellow filmmakers defenseless against my critiques: "I train real spies and they don't talk that way."

While riding through the compound, my fear was growing. I could feel the muscles in my face tightening, my body becoming rigid, my gestures getting stiff and mechanical and my smile forced. The driver asked about our work, and in responding I felt as though I was faking it.

The road came to a fork, and the driver stopped for a moment before making a decision. I half expected to see the Scarecrow from "The Wizard of Oz" with his arms pointing in both directions at once. We came out of the trees and were instantly "downtown." It was a mock city block, like the set of a movie studio, erected for training purposes. There were scores of police officers in riot gear and an angry mob of picketers shouting and throwing things at the cops.

> DRIVER: Wehire localactors to help ourguys practice riot-control techniques, and test out the new gear.

The actors looked pretty angry as they hurled objects at riot shields. I figured they were probably venting years of frustration over parking tickets. We drove carefully around them as smoke grenades clouded the road.

As we pulled through our checkpoint, the sound of gunfire built to a crescendo, indicating ample attendance on the firing ranges. The gate guard verified my badge, and then Mr. Spock's, and the driver pulled into a parking area to let us out.

> DRIVER: Don't be surprised if the ground shakes a few times after lunch. The ATF is blowing up cars today.

He let us out between two endless rows of tin Quonset huts, like the set of the TV show "Gomer Pyle, U.S.M.C." A familiar voice spoke in my head: "Well, gawwwwly! You have stage fright, don't you? Isn't that the opposite of what you teach? Surprise, surprise, surprise!"

Everything we are, and everything we become, is the result of how we present. We win our clients and our projects in presentations. We gain our employment through presenting ourselves during an interview. And most likely, those interviews happened because of the way we presented ourselves in networking. People listen to us, believe in us, finance us, follow us, notice us, select us, fall in love with us, agree with us, align with us and buy from us when we present well.

Most of us don't realize how often we present. Any time we communicate something we care about, share an idea, propose an action, draw a line in the sand or have a stake in an outcome, we're presenting.

Winning over these agents would require every version of presenting I could think of. The spotlight would be on us all day, and I was still in my cage. I knew I had to get out of it and accept the vulnerability in order to win.

At the training, I could sense a hostile audience who didn't like "artsy" types. Their body language indicated that this course seemed stupid to them. I flashed back in my mind to several years earlier—to a painful presentation I gave in my media promotions company. I was attempting to win over a room of prospects but I was scared and trying to hide it until a large drop of sweat blew my cover, skiing down my nose to land with a thunderous *thwap* on my notes. Today before the agents, I was temporarily paralyzed, stuck there, listening to my heartbeat pounding in my ears.

Few people actually like the experience of the hot seat that presenting creates. Even seasoned executives can crumble when you put them on a stage in front of a group of people. Some make it look easy, stepping comfortably into the role of presenter and moving ahead faster than anyone else because of perceived confidence and higher visibility.

As I stepped out before them, I drew a blank. I stood there, not remembering how to start. But I knew this wasn't a moment to merely survive—*this was a moment I needed to own.*

These tough-looking men and women looked impenetrable. I felt I had no choice but to match strength with strength, keeping my vulnerability safely locked away, but when I looked one of the agents directly into the eyes, what I saw surprised me.

He flinched.

It was a tiny tell, but suddenly I could see through the facade. That truth set me free to fly. *He had fear too.* I'd glimpsed the part of him he was hiding from me. Vulnerability was a terrifying idea to him. He believed that a glimpse of that would get him *killed!* I don't ever have to worry about "killed." If I did a bad job in a presentation, I might lose some business. If an actor I coached gave a poor performance, it might mean a bad review on the variety page. But this agent's "bad review" would be found in the obituaries. This yang-heavy tough guy was terrified of the yin he was hiding in the cage. And because of that, he was going to have a hard time playing his role undercover. He might be exposed as a cop.

Suddenly, getting out of the cage wasn't *my* problem—it was *his!* They were all going to be struggling to present and persuade authentically, because they were so practiced at *never* letting their guard down.

Authenticity is the prime directive in speaking, presenting yourself or going out on a limb to convince anyone to do, share or think what you want them to. It doesn't matter who you are. Powerful presence is authentic, and authenticity is an integration of strength and vulnerability. It's complete. It's all that you are, not half of it. It's not the eggshell with no egg inside. It's not hiding behind a mask or wearing a superhero costume. We teach screen actors that the last thing a performance needs is *acting*. We need "actual you" in a specified role.

With that realization, I wasn't there for me anymore. I was there for them, dealing with their emotional challenge of having packed everything fragile inside their protective armor. Suddenly the answers were coming to me again, and the dots were connecting between the agents, the work Pete and I had done with actors, and all the pitching, selling and leadership I'd done to run a company and direct a movie. I recognized that all of life is a stage, *and the people in front of me* had stage fright.

It all happened for me in that awkward silence before I spoke my first word. The chemistry of presence was a science I suddenly understood as I took one dynamic leap through the bars of my cage to take charge of that group using everything I was, with everything I had. Hours into the training, I still had them hanging on my every word.

I remember describing a hypothetical scenario for how the agents would leverage emotions to escape a dangerous situation, and one of the rookie agents challenged me outright by asking, "How would feeling sad ever save me on a mission?" It was a hard thing to answer confidently, having never been on a covert mission myself. I painted for him a scenario where you could use emotions like sad to convince someone that your made-up story was true, like pretending you got bad news and having the bad guys believe you and let you leave.

Suddenly, a veteran agent proctor stood up and interrupted me. "Dean, how would you have any idea if what you're saying would work at all in the field?" It was a scary spotlight of interrogation to point at any presenter. I was about to explain that while I have never done undercover work myself, I know people, and I stick to the truths I know regarding how they operate and communicate under pressure. But before I could do it, he continued with a statement I could never have seen coming.

"I ask because what you just described is exactly what saved my life back in '83, and I've been trying to find a way to articulate that ever since. Team, you better listen to what this man is telling you, because it will save your life too when you have no gun, no backup and only yourself to rely on."

He went on to tell a powerful story about infiltrating a dangerous group of criminals. He worked for months to "network" his way into the target group he was trying to infiltrate. Once inside, he had to work his way up the ranks to gain enough trust to access the top tier of the organization, after which he would have to secure enough evidence to bring them down.

As it happened, the bad guys were operating from an island somewhere off the grid and when this agent finally got on the inside, he had been blindfolded, put in the trunk of a car, driven for hours, then flown from inside the cargo section of a seaplane to the island. He had no idea where he was, or how to escape. But months before the day to which he was referring, he and his agent colleagues had come up with an escape plan. Since he knew that the secret headquarters was somewhere in the middle of nowhere, he assumed he could eventually locate a GPS and gain coordinates to his location. And when he had enough evidence to make a case, he would call an untraceable number and leave the camp's coordinates, after which the agents would find some way to get him a message to trigger his release from the island.

Eventually, he got enough evidence, found a GPS, and called in his longitude and latitude signaling that he was sitting on enough evidence to bring them down. For weeks he waited, knowing that the only way on or off the island besides the seaplane was a weekly supply boat that brought food to the camp.

One day, in addition to the usual supplies, the driver was carrying a letter for the agent, addressed to match the details of his cover role. The letter was given over to the crime bosses, who read it first, and then brought it to the agent, who was made to read it while they watched him.

"I knew the letter was a ruse, sent from my fellow agents who had a plan to get them to let me go," the agent proctor told us. "I was a little nervous because the most dangerous point of any mission comes when you've got enough evidence and you have to escape. Despite the stakes, I was feeling excited, and hopeful that I would soon be getting out of there. But as I read the letter, I realized my buddies' plan. The letter said that my father had died, and I had to find it in my performance right then and there to cry, and show them that this letter was authentic.

In those critical seconds of realizing that the only way I would survive would be to find my pure emotions and go through the sadness as if it were true, I realized how dangerous an idea this was. I knew my actual father had not died, but I had to find the vulnerable part of me and bring it forth and go through the correct emotions to authenticate the message.

At first, I didn't feel anything at all. And then I saw one of the thugs slide his hands deep inside his jacket where I knew he kept his gun. I thought of my wife, who I might never see again. I imagined how sad it would be for her if I never returned, and how long she had worried about this very thing.

Suddenly I touched the emotion, and pulled it to the surface despite the pressure I was under. I cried, and that's when I saved my own life. I knew it when the thug took his hand out of his jacket and put it on my shoulder to comfort me.

They sent me back on the supply boat, and I was free, because I had gone against my own instinct to hide my feelings. The part of me that was strong could never have given me the influence that vulnerability did. I was truly convincing, and I saved myself with sadness."

Standing there in front of those agents, having resisted my own urge to hold back, I now owned the room. My vulnerability became my strength. I had influenced them with my authenticity, and achieved exactly what my job required.

I was still as far away from home as I'd ever been but the sun was shining on me in this strange land because I had *all of me* to draw upon and I was not holding back. I had created a new partnership between my hard shell and the softness inside. They could work together far more powerfully than either yin or yang could hope to be on their own.

That was my story from stage fright to stage presence, and it led me to a whole new world beyond holding back. I had sensed its existence, but could not prove it to myself without giving up my hiding place. The courage to step out of it allowed me to train those rookie covert agents, and later to expand my public speaking career to the international stage. It helped me to coach high-pressure, competitive sales presentations that won over $2 billion in new business, including one single presentation worth nearly $350 million.

The skills you need to find your winning presence draw upon qualities you already have inside you. Some of what you need is already strong and practiced. Some of what you need is locked up and awaiting release so you can express your passion and authenticity without holding back.

The door to winning presence is open.
It's time to step through and seize center stage.

Chapter 1

The Fear in Your Way

> TIMO CRUZ: Our deepest fear is not that we are inadequate. Our deepest fear is that we are powerful beyond measure.
>
> *Script from the movie*
> "Coach Carter"

Sometimes the biggest thing in the way is not your lack of skills, but your fear. The fear that you feel can keep you from moving forward, or from even trying to move forward. It can affect your performance in the moment, and your willingness to perform in the first place.

The information in this book is for you if:

- You have fear
- Your presentations don't live up to their potential
- You lack confidence
- You are introverted
- You doubt your ability to influence
- You are already pretty good, and you want to go further

A Fate Worse Than Death

The resistance to presenting is shared across every industry. People fall somewhere on a continuum with some more afraid and others less so of stepping out of the fear that cages them. When my business partner Pete speaks on make-or-break pressure, he often quotes comedian Jerry

Seinfeld who made a great joke about public speaking that is based on results from an actual poll:

"A recent survey stated that the average person's greatest fear is having to give a speech in public. Somehow this ranked even higher than death, which was third on the list. So, you're telling me that at a funeral, most people would rather be the guy in the coffin than have to stand up and give a eulogy." (Source of quote: http://www.imdb.com/name/nm0000632/bio)

Clearly, some birds would rather die in their cages than live beyond them.

So, why does speaking in front of a group create more pressure than speaking to an individual? It's "group effect." If one individual has *presence*, a group has *mass presence*, amplifying an experience of *mass attention* through *mass eye contact*. Presenting can make you feel like an ant under a magnifying glass, the pressure stifling even the most animated of personalities, dampening your ability to make the positive impact you're absolutely capable of.

When every eye is on you, you can become unnerved. You feel the pressure coming from the audience and you know it's a moment that will be made or broken based on the *variable of your human performance.* Like a surfer riding a wave, the actual experience is a performance event. Many factors will play out in real time to determine outcome: the audience, the subject, the circumstances, your skills and experience, your attitude at that particular moment and the emotions coursing through you.

It is not unusual when we work with an organization that participants resist getting up in front of the group, even for the easy drills. We've had to wait as long as five minutes for a volunteer. But when we get one, success is usually instant, because developing the skill is the easy part. Resistance to discomfort is the substantial hurdle.

As Pete and I directed more people who had to perform under pressure, we found that the problem affecting performance wasn't necessarily the fear—it related more to how the emotion of fear redirected attention. Presenters doing really well reported that their focus was on their audience, their message and making a difference. Presenters reporting fear told us they were mostly aware of their heart beating, noticing sweat on their eyebrows or feeling their quivering knees.

When we asked what presenters were thinking about, the confident presenters were attending to the audience's progress and growth, while the fearful presenters were worried about their own standing with the audience.

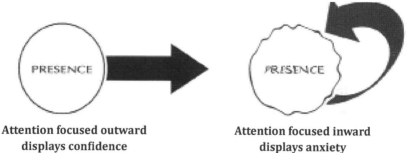

Attention focused outward
displays confidence
         Attention focused inward
displays anxiety

When we polled our presenters about their fear, it was no surprise that the fearful presenters reported a "pit in the stomach" feeling. The confident presenters were initially unaware of any fear. As we probed deeper, it was clear that they did have fear but they weren't paying attention to it. Our conclusion, which holds true today, is that attention, far more than fear, is the culprit of poor speaking presence. People experiencing fear *can be perceived as confident,* if they can point their attention in the right direction.

Fear isn't in your way.
Attention on yourself is the problem.
If attention is off of you, fear is not a problem.

Forget Perfection

One of the many things that holds you back is your seemingly hard-wired belief that the only good presenting is perfect presenting. The quest for perfection has sent many professionals far off track, pursuing something that can never be accomplished.

Striving for perfection can cause you to deliver less.

Think about when you watch presenters. Have you ever noticed that the more perfect the presenters get, the more "slick" they look and the less authentic they seem? If you ever do manage to achieve perfection, nobody will trust you. Hollywood knows this, which is why all the best characters are broken in some way. Sure, movie stars seem to pursue a fair amount of physical perfection, but filmmakers know that the likeability of their characters is in the mix of the character's fine and flawed qualities. These help the real people in the audience relate to them.

This is truly the little-known secret about presenting: The more perfect you are, the more untrustworthy you seem. Because perfect is inhuman. *The more authentically imperfect you are, the more believable you are.*

Keep this concept in mind: *Perfection is not the goal. Authenticity is.* Getting all your words out right is irrelevant. Losing your place and having to think for a moment is not a problem. *Being real, and in-the-moment is everything.* Don't let mistakes hold you back, especially when imperfections help others relate to you. *Authenticity is what the audience wants.* Bring your flaws up in front of the group and be real for them.

All of Life is a Stage, and We Have Stage Fright

It's not just getting up in front of a room full of people that causes fear. It's not just "public speaking" that's the problem. When you are presenting yourself in every aspect of your life—or at least you're trying to—fear is getting in your way.

At the moment you start presenting, you have nowhere to hide because your emotions are heightened and visible through your body language. In this case, those who:

- Attempt to hide from or deny their fears tend to be incapacitated by them
- Embrace their fears, come to enjoy the experience like a kid enjoying a roller-coaster.

Fear isn't a bad thing, but instead is a *performance enhancer.* You need to develop an *appreciation for your own fear*, and the role it plays in your courage. Instead of resisting or permitting it—value it, and enjoy it.

If you are like me, fear is the trigger for hesitation, yet it is also the energy that makes life exciting. If you embrace your fears, you become master of your own forward movement.

Choosing fear *changes* fear from adversity to adventure.

Even veteran actors have stage fright. Most realize that it is actually a good thing, keeping them primed with extra energy and faster processing. For them, fear is *part of the fun.*

Befriending Fear and Self-Doubt

Many of our clients come to us wanting to lose their discomfort, but we don't recommend that. We help them get comfortable with discomfort, so that they can move forward regardless of how they feel. That's our definition of courage: having fear and moving forward.

We strive to increase your courage so you can tolerate more discomfort and cross that scary line in the sand. It's an imaginary line anyway, and it's easier to cross than you think. We're going to show you how.

People who dread public speaking usually have the stuff it takes to be fantastic presenters because fear itself is one of the most powerful drivers of great stage presence. You may want to get past that fear, but if you're really lucky, you won't, and it will continue to drive you to higher and higher places. All you need to know is the secret of how to work with it.

Most people roll their eyes when they hear, "Be yourself and you'll be fine." The people who tell you that are technically right, but their advice is not complete. You can't act upon it or create a new outcome because they haven't told you *how* to be yourself under pressure. I had a would-be mentor tell me, "Use your anxiety in a positive way," and he suggested that I, "Convert the bad energy into good energy." These were correct ideas as well, but the missing link was always the method to do that.

So let me supply that missing link. I'm going to provide an approach that explains exactly how to:

- Be yourself naturally
- Channel anxiety into positive energy
- Be okay with fear
- Be natural under pressure
- Achieve winning presence consistently

All of our methodology is founded in basic human qualities, skills, aptitudes and experiences that *everyone* has. We use new and fresh combinations of skills we can count on already being there. These combinations will work if you embrace them. They are the key to:

- Better presenting
- Managing your emotions under pressure
- Connecting to people you need to influence
- Designing a presentation
- Speaking powerfully "on the fly"
- Thinking on your feet
- Responding to tough questions

Together, we will help you find your passion, discover your authentic self, and inspire others.

Why Does Fear Exist?

Fear exists to keep you safe. If you are feeling it, you're likely perceiving danger. The harder you try to silence the fear, the louder it will shout to protect you. The problem you run into is that it isn't always grounded in actual danger, so you need to spend time with your fear to evaluate when it justifies action and when it should be ignored.

Instead of pushing away from your fear, lean in and listen closely to what it wants you to know. Fear is nothing more than a warning buzzer in a sensitive alarm system. While being an integral part of your survival, it lacks the ability to tell the difference between real and perceived danger.

A coaching client of ours had developed a fear of fear itself. The experience of fear had become so repellant to him that he avoided it at all costs. As it happened, on the day we were meeting, his building's fire alarm system was being tested. When it went off it startled me, but not him. "Do we need to evacuate the building?" I asked when the buzzer sounded. "No worries," he said, "that's not a fire, that's just a fire alarm. It's been going off all day."

I realized that this was the perfect analogy for his fear. Fear isn't danger any more than a fire alarm is a fire. It is a heads up to the possibility of danger. It is asking you to check to see if the danger is real. So if you know there isn't any real danger, you don't need to react despite the noise it makes.

It was fun to watch his 'ah-ha' moment as I spelled this out for him. He realized that fear wasn't a problem—it was just an alert. And he recognized that he was wasting time reacting to what was only a possibility. He now views his fear like the alarm, knowing it is his responsibility to check before *deciding* if there is anything to fear or not.

Once he defined fear as only an indicator of potential danger, he created an amazing new relationship with fear, using it as a tool to navigate his progress. "If I feel no fear at all, I must not be reaching high enough," he explained, and began pursuing things that gave him the right amount of fear to confirm that he was pushing forward, but not too far. He told me he came to consider life more precious than it had been to him before, and his new relationship with fear helped ensure that he didn't waste a moment of it.

Fear is a good wake-up call. You neither want to assume the worst, nor disregard it entirely. That would be like ignoring a fire alarm without checking to see if there's a real fire.

When you walk through fear's doorway,
you have a chance to step into your greatest potential.

Walking Through Fear's Doorway

A woman came to us because she believed herself to be a fraud. She said, "I know my stuff, but I don't believe I'm a 'for real' speaker like my colleagues are." When asked why she felt so inadequate, she said it was because she was so fearful in front of audiences, while it seemed like her colleagues were nothing but excited to be in front of theirs.

In a single short session, we were able to solve this problem for her. We helped her see a pattern. She was experiencing a sudden burst of energy that is felt by everyone who presents, including her colleagues. But unlike her colleagues, she was resisting that energy. She was hating it and wanting to make it go away. So for her, the energy became *fear.*

Her colleagues, on the other hand, were using the energy to fuel their performance. They were actively embracing the energy, and recognizing it for the value it provided them. So for them, the energy became *excitement.*

Our client wasn't experiencing anything different than her colleagues were—they were all experiencing energy around presenting. She was just reacting to it differently—resisting the energy, instead of embracing it. So we gave her an experience of presenting while actively *appreciating* the energy, and she recognized how much better it felt. When we showed her how she *looked* while she was appreciating that energy, she saw that she looked just like her colleagues—the ones who were beaming excitement to be in front of their audiences.

This marked the end of her fraud complex. She knew she was legitimate, and now understood that her colleagues were not so fearless after all. They were struck with the same energy she was, they were just responding to it differently—appreciating it and embracing it, instead of resisting it. The fear was not gone. It was simply redefined, inside of her, but no longer in her way.

Summarizing Fear

Everyone has fear that they've been running away from for years. And it's been chasing them just as long. I once saw a cat with a balloon stuck to its back by static electricity. It was a hilarious sight, watching him try to run away from it. I'm sure my years of running from fear looked just as ridiculous.

If the cat had grabbed the balloon, it would have popped. When I grab my fear and pull it along with me, it pulls away from me. But I won't let it escape because I want my fear with me.

Fear is a useful alarm system that clues us in on possible danger.

It is a radar gun to gauge the speed of your forward movement. If you have no fear, it means you're not stepping forward fast enough. Too much fear, and you may be overstepping your readiness. But only you'll know

if your radar gun is calibrated correctly. With some practice, you'll find the sweet spot between moving too fast and not moving at all. Let your manageable anxiety be an indicator of progress.

Embrace your fear and self-doubt. When I reach the front of the line to the presenting roller-coaster, I lift the safety bar for these former arch-enemies, and buckle them in for a thrilling ride. I realize that *they* are the ones who are afraid. I am the one who has courage, because I am the one who chooses to go forward and bring them along. Courage isn't fearlessness—it *requires* fear. Courage is moving forward *with* fear. It's using the fear as fuel, to keep the roller-coaster exciting.

Chapter 2

Mastering Influence in Presentation

DR. IRIS HINEMAN: When the pressure is on, every creature on earth is interested in one thing and one thing only: Its own survival.

Script from the movie "Minority Report"

The number one distraction from influencing others is concern for your own survival. You find yourself up in front of a group and bristle against the experience, as though your very life was endangered. Then as quickly as possible, you race through your information so that you can return again to the safety of the group.

But presenting is not about survival. It's barely about you at all. It's about bringing value to an audience so that they will benefit. You're trying to influence them to do something, to learn something or to change in some way—to make something good happen. You speak in order to influence others.

Speaking for the very purpose of helping others is one of the best routes out of the cage. The armor you wear is all about protecting you from the people around you, so the intention to help the people you're trying to influence counters your need for self-protection. If you can commit to helping others when you present, communicate and persuade, you will shift your focus outward, reducing the need for self-protection, and freeing yourself to influence from the intention of mutual gain.

The people you want to influence are not your opponents if you've come to help them. With the mindset of helping, your audience isn't your enemy congregating to watch you fail. They are your fans, rooting for your success. They want to be convinced. They want your influence. They want to be persuaded.

Some of our SagePresence clients have challenged us on this point, claiming, "I'm not trying to influence anybody. I'm only attempting to deliver information." They're doing themselves and their audience a disservice when they take that perspective.

Every time you present, you must have a goal in mind. There has to be a reason to be speaking to a group. If you're not looking to make a difference with your words, then you're wasting everyone's time.

When you have a definite goal in your presentations, you are looking to generate a particular effect on your audience. Influence is the way to produce that effect.

A common reason to present is to influence others to view you as confident and impressive, to be perceived as more important. This may sound self-serving, but it's an essential ingredient in moving up within any team or community. In reality, it neither serves you nor the audience if your presentations are centered around making you look good. You need to influence to make a difference for them, not to dictate their perception of you. An effective presentation will produce a positive assessment of you, but that will be a secondary result, not a primary one.

Very often, the fact that *you want your audience to do something* gets in your way. It can be so much so that you hide from your own agenda. You pretend that you don't want to influence them, that you just want to give them the information so they can make their own decisions, but usually there is a result you want to obtain.

At the very least, if you are presenting, there's something you're saying that is *important to you*. If it's important to you then you feel the need to say the right thing in the the right way, whether at work, at home,or in your community. You feel pressure, and then hazards come into play.

You shape worlds by presenting your perspective and trying to influence others to support it. Presenting affects your marriage, friendships, career, recreation, long-range planning and ultimately your station in life. Whenever you're forming an argument and making your case—work-related, family issues or money matter—you are presenting. How you handle this experience determines what you go for or what you avoid. This is how you shape your own life.

Taking Responsibility for Both Sides:
The Presence of Influence

Influence requires that you embrace setting the tone for your interactions. You help people see specific things in certain ways, taking responsibility for guiding them to a better place. This is what influence is. It is your responsibility to make a safe environment for others to receive your influence.

It is important, when you want to leverage your stage presence to influence, to create a secure place for the people around you to express themselves authentically. And in every *unsafe* environment or one in which you or others feel vulnerable, you need to create a safe bubble in which to operate so that everyone involved can genuinely express themselves without holding back.

Influencing to Manifest Reality

As a filmmaker who fabricates fictional worlds and who also happens to be a speaker and trainer working in the actual world, I use reality to create fiction and fiction to create reality. I bring to life imaginary stories to capture real-world truths, and within the confines of the real world, I use stories to influence and manifest reality around me.

Together, these practices have helped me develop a creative relationship with the reality of my life. I'm not able to dictate all of the details of how my life goes. At best, I share control. But what I do is far more empowering than simply following the path of least resistance, like a leaf in a river.

My version of influencing reality begins with creating a win-win emotional tone in my environment. I use the power of story to organize and shape all the facts and details around me. That way, I am more likely to move toward my goals in an atmosphere more suitable for my growth.

In the past, presenting was a necessary evil, seemingly in the way of the things that I wanted. Leading up to that undesirable moment of trying to win over yet another person, I had the laborious task of crafting the right message.

Today, I view presenting as a practice of telling stories to win others over, one make-or-break moment at a time.

When influencing reality with presentation and story skills, the journey is more important than the destination. When you, your journey, and your communication align, you will touch many lives on your way to where you are going. You will help others in the process of getting what you want, just by achieving this alignment.

Influencing Yourself

The same processes used to present to others—the safe emotional tone, shaping messages with story—are practical skills you can use to *influence yourself.* The number one decision-maker who you need to influence the most, and the one specific individual who has held you back more than any other, is *yourself.*

Most people have a near-constant chatter in their minds. That chatter can talk you in and out of anything. When you're not trying to convince those around you, you are trying to convince yourself. The internal arguments that you make to yourself can benefit from the same presentation techniques you're using to influence others.

You regularly have competing thoughts bouncing in your mind, and you intellectually and emotionally present the arguments internally in order to decide. But you're seldom conscious of all the self-arguing you're doing. You get one idea to do something, and that triggers a competing idea about *not* doing it. Your mind becomes a battlefield, where two thoughts enter and one thought leaves, like a scene in "Mad Max Beyond Thunderdome." This is you, playing both the prosecution and defense, making your case and closing arguments until you persuade yourself to take action.

It makes me recognize that I am not entirely sure where the line is between *Me* and the thoughts that I have. I once had a mentor who told me, "If you can perceive something, then it must not be you." So I am separate from my thoughts, because I am able to notice them. I've learned to recognize when I'm having a thought that isn't serving me so I can separate myself from the thought and reduce its power. And I can choose a more positive thought. In this way, I have gained more control of both thoughts and feelings. For example, if I have a bad attitude, I can present to myself a different story and tone and actually influence myself to feel better without anything changing in the world around me.

You are not your thoughts. You are the one *having* your thoughts. And you are the one making decisions based on a mix of your thoughts and those voiced by someone else. View all communication with others, and internal chatter within your mind, in the same light. By organizing your thoughts and managing tone, you can influence others, and influence yourself.

Creating "Instant Authority"

When Pete and I started our business, even with some experience, we had very few credentials to justify what we were doing. We had some techniques we were working on, but not much of a track record on which to hang our running shoes.

But speaking made us visible and positioned us with instant authority. To an audience, a speaker has assumed credentials. Somebody must have selected us to speak so it was assumed that the event organizers deemed us to be qualified candidates, and very few people ever asked us about our background as we were building our reputations, simply because we were speakers.

Since our presentation skills were good—and we delivered value— audience members were impressed. Almost immediately, decision-makers who heard us speak approached us for coaching and training. They represented companies that needed to make the right pitch to earn multi-million dollar projects and contracts, and we had presented our way to those opportunities.

Whenever we had an idea for a new business angle that we wanted to try, we built a seminar around that idea. Next we spoke on the subject until we gained clientele, gradually building our track record. In that way, we presented our way to success, and the proof came to exist later.

Starting a Business

Not surprisingly, the same approach worked for our clients. When we taught them to present powerfully, they made themselves visible, increasing the perception in the eyes of their market that they were experts. You might call this 'fake it 'til you make it but I call it 'be it, 'til you see it.'

When we worked with a massage therapist who wanted to start her own business, we used this approach. We taught her to go into companies and educate employees on how to deal with and how to reduce stress in the workplace. In doing so, she would get the chance to offer massage therapy services to workers who were stressed out.

She began by offering free presentations at three major companies. People began to know and trust her. We advised her to give away some of her best knowledge on dealing with stress in the workplace. Showing her expertise landed her a few clients at each firm. Soon, she had enough clients to solidify her practice.

Changing Perceptions

This same approach worked very effectively in supporting a woman in middle management who was not perceived as a leader, yet wanted to be. We taught her how to present, which helped her quickly become more visible to the executives who were always looking for rising stars.

Peers began to see her as being in a higher position than they'd viewed her before. She was required often to speak at company events, and now she seemed to speak *as* the company instead of from within it. This changed the way everyone treated her. She became a real player at the firm and her career climb sped up dramatically as a result.

The Cornerstones of Presenting

At SagePresence, we focus on three cornerstones to make a pyramid of powerful stage presence that is useful to any form of presenting you might do. They impact every audience, regardless of size:

1. Recognize and master your ability to form a *connection* with an audience.
2. Structure your *message* to lead someone somewhere.
3. Deliver it with *dynamism* to engage and inspire.

This is the triad of skills that give you stage presence. The pyramid is a synthesis of:

1. Your mind, which strategizes, and composes your communications.
2. Your heart, which feels your communications.
3. Your body, which gives your communications expression.

Each of these can form a bond between presenter and audience when you speak, lead, sell, network, interview and negotiate your way through make-or-break moments.

With the skills of presence, you must also choose why you need these skills in the first place. Keep in mind what goal you have for these skills.

At the end of this book, we'll revisit the question of why you need these skills—what you want to accomplish once you have the presence, and the presenting skills we'll be building here together.

Mastering presenting is achieving a **connection**
with your audience, story-structuring a compelling **message**
and delivering it with **dynamism.**

Chapter 3

The Power of Connection

DOROTHY BOYD: You had me at hello.

Script from the movie "Jerry McGuire"

Even the perfect message delivered well may fail to reach its intended audience without a connection. A weak connection is like interference to your presentation, or worse, a dropped call. Listeners may catch the basic gist, but the impact is dramatically reduced without a true and clear connection.

You must connect with the people you're trying to influence in order to have impact. You've surely led conversations or presented to audiences where the other person—or an entire audience—isn't really listening. You've spoken on subjects you're passionate about without making your listeners feel it for themselves. You need a connection in order to influence.

The connections you generate with your audience fall on an experiential spectrum from virtually none at all, to something close to mind-sharing. When the 'click' happens, it's usually automatic and subconscious. Both sides are naturally being drawn closer to each other. Surely you've experienced an interaction where the click happened, freeing you to be yourself, to let loose and open up. You can feel the other person's increased willingness to listen and consider what you're saying.

Notice how the click with someone feels safe and comfortable. Isn't safety and comfort the reason we hide? A good connection has you outside your cage, expressing yourself and your views *comfortably.*

So maybe you're pursuing the wrong source of safety. Maybe the *connection* is a better source of comfort, because it can be found in the outside world. With it, you can feel safe even in the open.

Connection is a natural process, and the more you understand how it works, the more you can intentionally create safety outside yourself and share that safety with others.

What is a Connection?

You know when you have one, and you know when you don't. But what specifically a connection is remains a mystery. Or at least it did until now. At SagePresence we've isolated precisely what a connection is, and solved the puzzle on how to consciously and reliably connect whenever we choose.

When we created our training program for actors, we began exploring this notion of a deep and powerful link between people. In a scene, some actors were able to *seem* like they were brothers, sisters, lovers or friends, even though they weren't. The connectors in the group really lit up a scene, not only shining themselves but also triggering a glow within their fellow performers. Others who were not natural connectors tended to look like people reading lines from a script.

Rob Nilsson, our San Francisco film mentor, taught us that connection was a skill that could be intuitively grasped and forged on demand. This was critical to performance.

A key to Rob's process was a workshop exercise that he put his actors through, which forced them to practice "connecting" with each other. This was an ambiguous instruction by design. Rob would ask his actors to look into each other's eyes silently until they felt that they had *achieved* a connection, whatever that meant to them. This subjective process was instantaneous for some and time-consuming for others.

Ambiguous or otherwise, this process seemed to indeed create a palpable sense of two people connecting. You could actually see the moment it happened. For our purposes, it wasn't yet a reliable methodology, but it did create the click, and that seemed to make the difference between genuine performance and play-acting.

As we worked with it, Pete and I discovered that the same practice allows actors to connect with live audiences. It also helps them connect to a remote audience through a camera. If they connect with the camera (inanimate as it may be), they will connect with an audience who will view their performance later.

The biggest surprise was still to come. It was an eventual revelation resulting from asking actors to practice connections in their daily lives. The goal was to help them develop more control for stage and screen. Taking us up on our request, they told us that they had consistent experiences with people in all areas of their lives. They reported that there wasn't any difference between connections in reality and on the set—the experience was exactly the same.

Building on studies with Rob Nilsson and on our research on improvisational filmmaker John Cassavetes, we workshopped and experimented to develop a methodology that reliably builds connections. To be clear, we didn't invent connection. We just came up with a model that allows you to understand what happens naturally, so you can intentionally and reliably ignite a connection.

The Million-Dollar Reason to Make a Connection

The management of a professional practice came to us with an urgent need. They were faced with arbitration. A very angry client was asking for a million dollar refund for unsatisfactory project completion. At the point we were brought in, the situation had escalated to a two-day arbitration to legally determine if the professional practice would have to refund the money. Mistakes were indeed made, but $1,000,000 would be devastating on top of losing a client that had been a great source of business for years.

We worked with the team to help them face the arbitration in the best possible way. They were very good at their job, but they brought us in because this challenge was way out of their comfort level and experience. Both companies were preparing for battle, and our team knew that their angry client was ready for the fight. When our clients entered the courtroom, they were met with what they described to us as "a wall of hate."

The secret we had taught them was how to connect, not fight. Instead of rising to battle, this team started making connections with members of the other team, appreciating all their collective years of great projects together. Within 15 minutes, our clients felt the wall of hate go down, and the hostility level lower dramatically.

Within the first hour, somebody on the "angry" side admitted, "Well, we made some mistakes too." By the second hour, the two sides were sharing ownership in what went wrong. The discussions ended at noon of the first day. The dollar settlement came in at about five percent of the original demand. More importantly, they protected a valuable 10-year client relationship, and they still do business with them to this day.

Seven concrete truths about connections explain the results our client achieved that day, including what precisely a connection is, how it works and what it takes to create one. Here they are:

TRUTH #1: A connection is an emotional experience shared by exactly two people.

Some interactions are basic information exchanges and others are an experience. A connection is the shared experience of a moment. When information is *felt,* it becomes an experience. To be an experience, emotion has to be part of the mix. Without emotion, it's just information.

Our definition of a connection is *strictly* a connection between one person, and exactly one other person. You can create the experience of a connection with a group, but strictly speaking, there *is no connection between a speaker and a group, except through one person at a time.*

TRUTH #2: A connection is forged with nothing more than attention and eye contact.

As mystical as the sought-after connection is, forging one is really pretty straightforward. If you put your attention on someone, and let him know your attention is on him with eye contact, the connection forms naturally, and emotions begin to flow between both of you.

Attention and eye contact are not the same. We at SagePresence believe that reaching out with eye contact is an action that says you are offering your undivided attention. How many times have you given someone your eye contact, only to think about other things while letting them talk? In networking when you do that, you might be thinking about what you're going to say next or who you would rather be talking to.

So you're not listening, but pretending you are, which is a nonverbal lie. And the other person *does* pick up on that lie, and it hurts his or her feelings.

This is a communication classic between married couples. A wife can usually tell exactly when her husband has drifted off and is thinking about something else. She will be talking and he will be nodding when suddenly she will don a condescending smile like Lois from the TV show, "Malcom in the Middle." She'll stop talking (this should be a "heads up"), put one hand on her hip, and ask, "What did I just say?" He is caught completely off guard, having been lost in thought long enough to qualify for a "missing- time incident." His eye contact promised her his attention, but he was completely busted for the nonverbal lie. His body language gave him away.

Attention without eye contact can create problems as well, like when listening to a co-worker without ungluing your eyes from your computer screen. In a world where attention is so scattered, it's a gift to actually give someone your undivided attention.

So imagine the communicative power when you give someone both your attention *and* your eye contact. It will probably inspire them to do the same back to you, and at that point, whatever your goal, a true connection has been established.

TRUTH #3: Emotions flow through connections, affecting both people.

Thoughts do not traverse a connection. No amount of eye contact and attention will telepathically communicate a meeting time or phone number. But if you feel sad while you are talking with someone, the other person will recognize it instantly, even if you say happy things. People can detect when you're masking an emotion, and can usually tell when you have good news to share, even before you share it. And if you are angry, but choose not to voice it, they still know, and the discomfort will flow back and forth between both of you through the connection.

Connections communicate emotions. How you feel when you share a connection will determine how that connection feels. Imagine the power of feeling confident when interviewing. If you feel confident, the other person will feel your confidence, and will view you accordingly.

Sound travels more effectively through water than air, and emotion travels most effectively through a connection. This is why you might subconsciously avoid connections, because deep down you know that you are making yourself transparent. It's also why you *want* a connection—to inspire your audience to feel something—which adds *inspiration* to the experience. Happy, sad and mad mix in as many ways as green, blue and red mix in the light that colors our world. As your emotions shine on the other person, you affect him or her. That person's emotions shine back at you too. The emotions of the two people in a connection mix, forming an experience that's larger than the individual feelings alone. Chemistry is the real-time experience of two people's feelings affecting each other.

TRUTH #4: Appreciation is the universal connector.

In acting class, we would practice different methods of forming a connection, and many approaches worked when given enough time. Eventually, we noticed that whenever two people achieved the click, they looked *appreciative*. So we tried making appreciation the activity itself, and suddenly the time required to connect went from minutes to seconds. Appreciation seemed to universally bond people with a number of interesting by-products:

1. **Appreciation increased comfort.** Imagine how uncomfortable it might be to stand right in front of another person, make eye contact without speaking and stay there silently for minutes on end. When we asked our actors to do this it made a lot of them wildly uncomfortable. But when we asked them to appreciate the other person, the tension subsided or reduced.

2. **The appreciative person tended to develop a "warm glow."** The person shifted from squirmy to an apparent calm. Next, he or she warmed up, and appeared more positive and caring. This soothing presence calmed the other person, while it invited him or her to share that emotional space.

3. **In their own words, people "forgot about themselves and saw the other person for the first time."** When we heard this, our real learning was about to unfold, and it led us to recognize the next big truth about connections.

TRUTH #5: Our feelings aren't really in our way.

Up until this last revelation—that when we appreciate someone else, we tend to lose track of ourselves—we had been under the impression that *feelings were getting in our way*. We believed that the negative feelings themselves were the problem, and that they were degrading our presence. But we now realized that the negative feelings weren't in our way at all, it was where our attention was that was the problem.

Even experienced actors can slip into the trap of paying too much attention to themselves, and when they do, their self-awareness will trigger a moment of panic, causing them to draw a blank. It's like throwing a circuit breaker somewhere between their head and their heart, shutting down the whole system.

It's the same with athletes. To win, a skier has to "lose herself in the slopes," or a golfer must "become one with the game," keeping their attention off themselves. When they fail, they are paying too much attention to their technique, or are hyper-aware of their bodies.

The enemy is not feelings. The pivotal determinant of presence is *where attention is focused!*

When you present, and your attention is on your audience or your content, your presence will climb. But when it's on yourself, it will suffer. You will notice how hard your heart is beating, you'll feel your sweat and how hot your cheeks are and wonder if you're blushing. This will certainly trigger self-doubt and more nagging questions about how the audience is viewing us.

There you stand, in front of everyone, all eyes upon you. And you, under fluorescent light, are scrutinizing yourself in an imaginary mirror. You're not happy with what you see. All you are aware of is yourself, and you don't *like* yourself at that moment.

But when you appreciate your audience, your attention will move off of you and onto them. You can't appreciate them if you're paying attention to yourself, and you can't pay attention to yourself when you're appreciating. So the very act of appreciating moves the attention to where it should be.

And more importantly, the *tone* of the attention you're giving is *positive* when you are appreciating. If you have fear, appreciate your audience. Your body language will follow the appreciation. The appreciative tone is absolutely magnetic. If you don't believe this, try appreciating a person you're talking to, and watch them change. They will soften, warm up, perk up, maybe smile, maybe nod, and if you don't see that change, I guarantee you'll *feel* it.

TRUTH #6: One simple question generates appreciation.

In every kind of situation, all you need to appreciate is this one question: *What do I appreciate about this person?* Your mind, especially with some practice, will do the rest in less than a second.

When we at Sage Presence began asking that question and testing the consistency of the responses, the results were beyond powerful. When you ask this question, your brain instantly gives you an answer.

Right now, look up from these words, and look at whatever *thing* is in front of you and ask yourself, "What do I appreciate about this thing?" It might be a thermostat, a chair back or a piece of art on the wall. If there's a person in the room, it will be even easier.

I happened to be alone, so I asked myself what I appreciated about the chip in the paint on the door trim, and what came to me was how much I appreciated the relative ease of fixing flaws with *paint*. In a world where so many things are hard, painting is one thing that's relatively easy, and I appreciate that. When I thought it, I could *feel* it. It wasn't deep appreciation, but it was definitely positive, and my attention immediately went off myself. This works with anything. Try it with a person, and it will be notably deeper.

That's how easy it is to resolve the fear factor that weakens your presence in the spotlight. Ask yourself what you appreciate about whoever is in front of you, and you'll be able to manually move your attention off of you, and onto the other person. Plus, you'll have a positive vibe.

Try practicing appreciating things, situations, and people with enough regularity that you can find the switch to move your attention in any scenario. Appreciating people will be the most common application, because you have face-to-face interactions all the time, and you're going to want to win people over in these interactions. For photo sessions, or recording yourself on video, the ability to appreciate the camera will be the most important key to on-screen presence.

We've taught clients to successfully use appreciation to take the focus off themselves in any number of make-or-break scenarios. It's worked in courtrooms, in networking, in front of a camera, when closing a sale, in negotiations, in the middle of an argument and when trying to recover from saying the wrong thing.

Often we are asked, "How can I appreciate someone I don't know?" People *think* they need something in common to appreciate someone. But you don't. If you've ever said hello to a person you're passing on a sidewalk, you must recognize the potential to appreciate people you don't know. Appreciate them for being there. That alone will create something in common. Surely they appreciate that they're there, too. Better yet, jump your mind to the concept that no man is an island—we are all one. If we are all one in humanity, the common denominator is already there.

All you have to remember is this question: What do I appreciate about this person?

TRUTH #7: Appreciation neutralizes fear.

Professional coach and emotional intelligence specialist Cheryl Alexander has been working from the premise that you can't feel both fear and appreciation *at the same time*. She has used this conviction to coach leaders to appreciate under pressure.

When you literally appreciate your fear, it changes to excitement. When you appreciate people who scare you, you will feel more confident.

It doesn't really matter what it is that you appreciate. General, specific, deep, or superficial, appreciation changes how you feel to something warm and positive. It neutralizes the fear reaction and any negative impact to your presence.

A Professional Case for Connection

I was in court in an important case. As a key witness in a case where I cared about the outcome, the stakes were high for me. I had been told to prepare to be on the stand for 45 minutes. Only five minutes into the process, I was floundering nervously.

My fear of authority kicked in and I found the courtroom a scary environment. Everything that I had to share I had powerfully delivered before. As I testified, it was sounding lame when it really counted. My voice had this little crackle like when I was eight and about to cry. I remember feeling that I didn't have enough air to breathe—I was sucking wind between sentences— and I looked at the floor when I answered.

As if the room, the judge and the jury weren't pressure enough, the other team's lawyer was very scary, and he kept coming at me with a stern hostility and penetrating, laser-beam eyes like the Terminator.

Plants in the corners of the courtroom wilted under his radiant hate-rays.

He also had another quality. Do you remember the "Columbo" TV show? Columbo seemed super-friendly on the outside, but at the last minute he'd turn around and say, "Oh. One more thing," and he'd ask the bad guy a single fatal question, and bring him to his knees.

Columbo's questions seemed benign enough, but he had been carefully calculating the facts like a card-counter at a gambling table in Vegas. His brilliance was cloaked under a clumsy act, so you wouldn't see the web he was weaving. This lawyer had that same quality, and

I felt like I was being set up for an unavoidable trap. As he mixed in a little Columbo with his Terminator act (the Columbinator?), I felt very vulnerable and it was dramatically affecting my presence. This man also had a way of repeating what I said as though it were absurd.

Quietly under the judge's radar, he was focusing an intense amount of anger at me, acccusing me in a defiant tone, cloaked in a calmly professional disguise. He looked so confident and sinister and I was playing right into his hands.

In reality, this was a performance to weaken my presence, so I seemed less credible. I remember actually starting to doubt my own recollection. The *truth* was starting to sound implausible to me, because he was so convincing in his suspicious act. This was causing me a lot of second-guessing, and self-editing, leading me to stammer.

Thankfully I pulled my act together, regained my composure, confidence, passion and presence. I remembered all of my points, and I endured the grilling on the stand so well that he cut me off early because I was doing too much damage to his case.

How did this change occur? I started appreciating his evil Columbo impersonation. I started appreciating how good he was at this job. And as I appreciated him, bless his heart, he was starting to like me too, despite the damage I was doing to his case by having great presence under pressure.

I won in court, and a month or so later, I bumped into the Columbinator at a networking event. The moment he saw me, he headed my way, as though I were a friend. But on the way across the room, he started to remember who I was. His steps got a little jerky and hesitant, but he seemed to recover by the time he got to my side of the room. He handed me his card and said, "I know we were on opposite sides of the courtroom that day, but I really enjoyed working with you nonetheless. If you're ever in my neck of the woods, I'll take you to lunch."

As I watched him walk away, I realized that I had the power to build rapport under pressure, even in battle. I had earned his respect, and now he actually liked me.

> *"Am I not destroying my enemies when I make friends of them?"*
> *—Abraham Lincoln*

From Stage Fright to Stage Presence in Three Phases

Pressure can make it hard to think clearly. So we needed to come up with a method of recovering from pressure so strikingly easy that you actually remember it even when stress peaks. This method allows you to:

- *Win* over key decision-makers
- *Set the stage* for effective selling
- *Build* relationships when you network
- *Bond* with teams you lead
- *Nurture* collaboration out of disagreement
- *Interview* with a sense of partnership

You typically go through three phases in make-or-break moments. It is important that you gain a clear understanding of all three. But the one to master is the third one—the one that accomplishes your goal of making a solid connection.

Let's look at each phase.

PHASE ONE: Just "Be"

The first thing to do in a make-or-break moment is to simply "Be."
Be yourself. Be however you are. Be nervous, confident, squirrelly or
whatever. Check in with yourself and see how you are feeling right now.
Try not to judge it; just recognize it for what it is and be in it without
trying to change it.

When my clients were walking into that million dollar arbitration
discussed earlier, they told me they checked in and noticed how it felt.
They had a "pit-in-the-stomach" feeling, as they approached the wall of
hate. They had to notice it before they could change it.

In our workshops, we ask participants to break into pairs, and stand
in silence before their partner. We have them face the other person
without talking...for about a minute. This creates an awkward, nervous
energy that most people describe as anxiety. They squirm, wanting to do
something about it. We think this is a close simulation to the pressure
of a make-or-break moment. The anxiety is begging for a decision, and
wondering which is necessary: *Fight* or *flight.*

PHASE TWO: Check Out

This is an interesting activity as it essentially calls for the opposite of a
connection. Imagine you're a radio. Experiencing anxiety is like static.
Phase One—where you "Be"—is like turning the volume loud. Here, in
Phase Two, we're having you turn the volume down.

Checking out reduces anxiety so that you can zero in on the
connection you want. All you have to do is shift your attention to
something other than the source of anxiety, maybe imagining you are
somewhere else, like relaxing by the fireplace.

In our workshops, we ask participants to imagine that the person
facing them is a window, and we have them look right through that
person and see something on the other side. Pete likes to point them

toward a "to-do" list. I have them imagine themselves alone, looking through a bedroom window at their lawn. Wherever they go, most people seem to be able to distance themselves easily from the pressure of the make-or- break moment by checking out. The actual situation hasn't changed, but anxiety has dropped.

This should tell you that you have more control than you thought within the make-or-break moments that cause so much pressure.

PHASE THREE: Connect

You've noticed and accepted your natural reaction to make-or-break moments by *being.* Then you felt a second of relief by *checking out.*

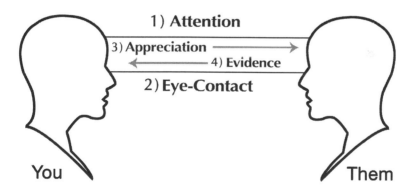

Connection Step 1:
Put your undivided attention on the other person.

In our workshops, we ask our participants to check back in, notice the person in front of them and give that person their undivided attention. This time there is no nervous body energy like there was in the "Be" phase. They are in the exact same situation that made them squirm just a few seconds ago, but having checked out, and checking back in with intention, they now seem to be calm and confident. The calm is the result of intentionality—they are *choosing* to face off with their partner this time, so it seems more under their control.

This is what I did in court with the Columbinator. After noticing my fear, I checked out for a second, before returning to the moment and putting my attention on him, instead of where he had put it—on me.

Connection Step 2: Eye Contact

Let the other person know your attention is on them by making eye contact. Steps 1 and 2 often happen together. We want to make these two distinct concepts. Offering undivided attention is a mental activity of focusing your awareness on someone. Eye contact is the body language that communicates we're doing this. When both are in place, we form a connection.

In the courtroom, I had been looking at the floor, over people's heads or to my own attorney because that felt safer. Now I was looking the Columbinator right in the eyes.

Connection Step 3: Appreciate within the connection.

All we have to do if appreciation isn't coming is ask ourselves, "What do I appreciate about this person?" Appreciation for the Columbinator wasn't coming automatically. Seconds earlier I hated the guy because he was so aggressive and intimidating. But I knew I needed to appreciate him, so I asked myself the question and got an instant answer. "He's pretty good at this," my mind shot back. Then I thought how hard it must be to do his job day after day. While I spend my days building people up, he has to tear people down all the time. So I kind of felt sorry for him.

I transitioned from fearing for myself to empathizing with, and admiring, a man who had a hard job and was good at it.

In our workshops, we ask participants to find one specific thing about the other person they can authentically appreciate. What that is varies from how they look, to what they wear, to how they smile, to them being a fellow human, to the way they share the awkwardness together. They all find something, and you can see their appreciation glow like a sunrise. All their anxiety gets replaced by winning presence.

People in Step 3 can also look *commanding.* People who are appreciating in the face of a challenge appear like leaders, because *this is what leaders do.* They find the positive at the end of a challenging negative and they light the way for their team.

Connection Step 4: Look for evidence of appreciation reaching the other person.

Check if you can see any sign on the other person's face that your appreciation is landing. This is usually, but not always, pretty visible. Classically, men show this less than women, but with practice you can detect it even when the signs are subtle.

There will probably be evidence of change even when you're appreciating someone who is angry or hostile towards you. In my courtroom experience, the evidence was instant. The Columbinator became less harsh toward me. His anger level dropped, and his face and voice seemed to soften. It's hard to hit a guy who's admiring you.

Day-to-day interactions are no different. Watch for the signs. You should be able to see the appreciation land. How the interaction plays out should also be affected in some positive way.

In our workshops, people report seeing smiles, or sudden depth and caring. Some say they could simply *feel* a difference. The bottom line is that they achieved the connection they desired.

Connection Summary

The more you practice *attention, eye contact, appreciation* and looking for *evidence*, the more automatic and instantaneous this process will become. You will be able to connect to a group of any size in about five seconds, and you'll do it by one random audience member at a time.

In one-on-one conversations, you'll be able to forge relationships in moments.

Connecting to an audience is appreciating them with attention and eye contact, one individual at a time. Connection is a system that is fueled by *appreciation*. It's a process of locking attention and eye contact to pull you and one other person together in a space where chemistry can happen. The chemistry is the mixing of emotions felt by the people involved. And by intentionally beaming appreciation through the connection, you can positively lead the tone of the interaction.

Connection will:

- Change your relationship with pressure
- Relieve you of fear around other people's negative emotions
- Attract others to you
- Create chemistry with those you're trying to influence
- Elevate your ability to lead and inspire
- Give you charisma

Connection works!

Chapter 4

From Connection to Chemistry

JEAN PAUL CLEMENT: Most people
are together just so they are not
alone. Some people want magic.
I think you are one of these
people.

Script from the movie
"Broken English"

The difference between informing someone and compelling them comes
down to the sparks that fly. If you have chemistry with people, energy
between you escalates. Without it, only information transfers and your
only hope is that the content will somehow ignite something powerful.

We start with the connection process because we want the conditions
to be right for sparks. The first condition required for sparks is *being
open.* There is no connection when you've insulated yourself from others.
Vulnerability is most definitely a part of the chemical equation, because
you have to be well beyond your cage door in order to interact with
anyone else.

Fortunately, connection creates a feeling of safety and trust to make
an emotional exchange possible. Once a connection is in place, it's time to
take it to the next level. *We want chemistry so that we can inspire.*

One person has presence.
Two people share chemistry.

When there's chemistry between a speaker and a crowd, that chemistry is created when the speaker connects with individuals in the group, one person at a time. Chemistry is a two-way street. Both people affect each other with their emotions. Whoever sustains his or her own emotion longer inspires the other and leads the exchange.

Once I was feeling playfully romantic at a time my wife was angry with me. One of us was going to change the mood by inspiring the other. Who inspired whom would decide whether we would fight, or pop the cork on a bottle of wine.

It could have gone any number of ways when our emotions mixed, but I stuck with my playfulness, and eventually saw the tiniest hint of a smile. She wanted to stay mad at me. But she couldn't—and finally she burst out laughing and I went for the Bordeaux. I inspired her to feel what I was feeling mostly because I held onto my feelings longer. I was pouring more of my playful energy into the emotional mixing pot than the amount of anger she was pouring into it.

In the same way, you can hold onto your passion and conviction as a speaker. You can outlast the audience. They may be bored with your topic, too busy for a presentation, or skeptical about something you're saying. Audiences seldom start out excited about any presentation. But they will follow you, based on the way you feel more than the things you say. If you can stay fired up, *regardless* of how the audience is responding, you can bring them to a feeling of inspiration eventually. As the speaker, your job is to lead the chemistry.

The magic of chemistry is actually stacked equally between the presenter and the audience. The speaker brings a lot of energy. Each of the audience members has less power as an individual listener, but together they command an equal energy to the speaker. Both the speaker and the audience share the power to inspire the other. The speaker can inspire the audience to get passionate or apathetic about the subject, and the audience can inspire the speaker to confidence or doubt.

Fortunately, the connection process makes the environment safe for both parties, so once you've formed appreciative connections within your audience, all you have to do is pump passion into the connections, and you'll be leading the chemistry. Too many presenters fear the emotional power of the audience so they unwittingly buy into presenting tricks that *reduce* chemistry: looking over people's heads instead of making eye contact, imagining the audience in their underwear or hiding behind a PowerPoint as its narrator. More commonly, it means putting your feelings in neutral and creating numbness to avoid emotional risk. You fear being negatively inspired, so you check out emotionally to protect yourself. You then experience some kind of win by virtue of the "zero loss." You didn't embarrass yourself, get rejected or lose any ground. But you sacrificed the potential of positive gain that lies beyond your emotional hiding place where risk and influence reside.

Two people mixing their emotions within a connection is like a beaker in a chemistry laboratory. Experiment with the chemicals, and you'll discover inspiration. With practice, chemistry can be within your control, and it can electrify your presentation.

Emotional chemistry is your biggest opportunity to differentiate yourself from other presenters, and your best chance to inspire your audience to care.

Chemistry and Social Media

In today's society, both on the business and personal level, everyone is connected by technology—some people 24/7. I think electronic communication is popular because it lets you communicate from the comfort of solitude. Messages are safety-stripped of body language signals so most of the risk is left outside the exchange. You won't get eye contact in an email exchange. There's no subtle head tilt in a Facebook post, no facetious tone in a text message and no cynical smile or guarded posture in a blog, unless it's written out intentionally.

Electronic communication is delayed. You post alone, and later you read a reply someone else made in seclusion. You can reach exponentially more people over the Internet, but you do so in isolation, where it's harder to form genuine chemistry.

People *require* important body language data in order to accurately interpret messages. Without it, the mind fills it in. Texts and emails seldom include the subtle emotional content that body language effortlessly communicates, leaving a lot to fill in for the reader. How many times have you misinterpreted an email's message as being angry, just because it was short?

In conversation, if people spoke as bluntly and emotionlessly as the average text, we'd all have a lot of hurt feelings. Messages stripped of emotional content sound blunt and snippy. When I received an email that read, "Proposal incomplete. Call ASAP!" I thought I was in trouble. As soon as my heart stopped pounding, I called the client. To my surprise, I found that my proposal was well-received, and they desired some more information. The sender had thumb-texted from the clumsy phone keyboard, so she sent only what she considered the "relevant information," which lacked the emotional content I needed. This wasn't chemistry—it was more like anti-chemistry.

Whether you're speaking or sending a text, your audience wants to know two things:

1. What are you saying to me?
2. How should I take it?

In texts and emails, abbreviations like LOL and emoticons like :) can go a long way toward communicating how we feel and and they help fulfill the message's intent. I recommend you articulate the emotional content with words, punctuation or emoticons. "Glad to get proposal! Reaction good. Have recommendation. Call when U can. Thx." That wasn't too hard. This version had an exclamation point, the word "glad," an invitation and a thanks, even though it was short.

Face-to-face communication is the ideal model for communicating, because verbal and physical, nonverbal communication allow for chemistry. Recognize the incredible gift of emotional communication that gets provided by nonverbal language. When body language is absent, be doubly careful to modify your words so that your audience perceives your message the way you intend it.

Leading an emotional exchange
is the single most powerful way to inspire another person.

Chemistry is More Than the Sum of the Words Spoken

The very *point* of a connection is to participate in the chemistry. That is where the richness of human interaction is experienced, and where you can have the most influence. Chemistry actively accelerates the information exchange, saying more than the sum of the words spoken.

Two people can silently connect on a glance, read and react to each other, both communicating without so much as a peep during one of those, "Are you thinking what I'm thinking?," moments. My wife and I communicate nonverbally quite well, and my business partner Pete and I regularly read each other in tag-team presentations, course-correcting and anticipating each other when there's no way to talk things over.

The Speaker's Paradox

Chemistry requires tolerating vulnerability, because you will likely feel unprotected when you allow yourself to experience emotions in front of others. Even while presenting to groups, you will gradually get used to feeling transparent and exposed. Eventually, you will generate excitement from this feeling of vulnerability, and become driven to inspire others.

Embracing the rush that vulnerability provides will help you create chemistry inside of a connection so your audience can experience what you're feeling.

Feeling your words is how you can inspire others to care about what you care about.

This is the public speaker's paradox: You naturally hold yourself back in front of others, yet emotional transparency is required to inspire. Emotional restraint seems socially safer, and offers *comfort*. Expressing freely seems socially dangerous, but it offers *influence* beyond it.

When you push yourself across that line—from holding back to expressing—you will find most of what you have been resisting is *merely discomfort* and not actually dangerous. While danger is imagined, your performance is real. When you're presenting, use appreciation to increase your comfort, so you can stay in the hot seat and express yourself.

With an appreciative connection established, you are free to move on to other feelings. If you practice being open to feeling your words, your content will automatically inspire you with different emotions, and that will dynamically inspire your audience.

Payoffs for Tolerating Vulnerability

Few of us will ever defeat vulnerability, but anyone can choose to *embrace* it. This brings big payoffs, including more excitement and a renewed sense of courage. Fearless presenting would be like hockey with no opposing team, or basketball with a hoop you could reach without jumping. Without vulnerability, you'd have no drive for continuous improvement.

Vulnerability leads to continued growth, excitement and fun.

The feeling of vulnerablity holds everyone back to some degree, so with every incremental increase, you will stand a head taller in the crowd. You'll discover you have no need to claw your way to the top when you can *feel your way there* with a simple understanding of how emotions work, what they're for and how they apply to a business setting.

The Function of Emotions

Look at emotions from the perspective of utility. One use I've discussed is to *inspire*, and the value of that is increased *influence*. Emotions serve other functions as well, bringing considerable value to human communication.

■ Emotions Validate Our Words

Emotions tell audiences that what you say is true, or at least that you believe it is. Audiences know a critical distinction exists between appearance on the *outside*, and truth on the *inside*. They want confirmation that the speaker is sincere.

People who mean what they say and have good intent behind their actions are trusted. Audiences accept a speaker they interpret to be genuine and reject a speaker who they suspect to have ulterior motives. A conclusion about integrity results from reading the speaker's emotions. Is she truly feeling her words when she says them? Does he *really* care?

Sincerity is the key to winning audience trust. You have to mean what you say and say what you mean. If a speaker claims to be driven by the desire to help you, but you sense he is only in it for your money, you will reject him. If you believe a speaker to be genuinely driven to help you, then you won't mind *if* he gets rich in the process. Surprisingly, you'll also accept a speaker who is all about the money if he comes out and says so. Promises need to match intent, and your audience will size you up based on a comparison of what you say, and how you feel when you say it.

Regardless of what you're selling, your audience is going to scrutinize the consistency between your words and your emotions to reach a conclusion about your integrity.

You want to be emotionally aligned to what you're saying when you speak to your audience. Everyone today is bombarded with dynamic messages, big promises and an overwhelming number of claims. People are sophisticated and look for any disparity that will help them reject an offer. What is the message? What is the intent? Does the presenter really mean it?

How can you be sure to show your audience that you mean what you say, and that your intent is forthright? A great start is to make sure in your presentation, you:

- Have good intent
- Are up front
- Mean what you say
- Speak from an ethical position of integrity
- Work toward improving and being more completely understood
- Commit to having a win-win intention
- Feel your emotions authentically

People are head-heart-action machines. They think, and also *feel*, which together lead them to *act.* Those three work together to create the human experience, and when aligned, powerful communication occurs and people trust it.

*In photography, **seeing** is believing.*
*In presenting, **feeling** is believing.*

When I present, I give you no choice but to believe in me. I don't win over *everyone*, but I win over the vast majority of people—reliably and consistently. I even succeed with some who disagree with me. This is not because I'm particularly gifted in articulating my message, nor is it because my content is so powerful that you couldn't possibly resist it. I succeed because *feeling is believing,* and I'm willing and able to feel in front of you. You will know my intentions because I will state them, and you'll know that I mean it because you'll see that I feel it. You will read my genuineness through my body language, and likely feel to some degree whatever I am feeling. Because I'm making direct eye contact with you, we will experience each other's emotions and together amplify our passion for the topic.

■ Emotions Give Your Audience an Experience Beyond Words

Magic words are really plain words experienced emotionally. When you feel your words, you put the magic into them by triggering feelings in your audience. When emotions are present, your audience is going to experience more than the information, and it doesn't really matter if the emotions you intend to trigger are actually the ones felt. Filmmakers know that the bottom line is most definitely that the audience feels *something.* The only true failure is when your audience feels nothing.

Information is good—but inspiration is magic.

Emotional experience can be overt or subtle. Feelings are scored more on a pass/fail system, and less on a curve. They're either there or they aren't, and your only reliable method of creating them is to *feel them* into existence.

■ Emotions Emphasize

Have you ever heard someone tell a secret? He leans in with the tiniest hint of a devilish smile, and speaks in a soft, covert voice. He hasn't even said the word secret, but his body language is telling you that he knows something and he's going to spill it. Emotions are at work here, emphasizing the significance of something that hasn't even been said yet. It's all in the way he *felt* when he said it that pulled your focus toward the intrigue of his secret.

This is emotional emphasis. If you say something with emotion, any emotion, it's going to differentiate itself from everything else you have said. An audience listening to a speaker who feels emotions will automatically experience highs and lows, whereas a group listening to an emotionless speaker will have a very flat experience. You don't have to plan out the emotions. Open yourself up to feeling your words, and your emotions will naturally emphasize what you most want your audience to hear.

■ Emotions Bend Meaning

Read between the lines, and what you'll be reading is emotion. Feelings are the substance between the lines, the color in what would otherwise be a black-and-white line drawing. They bend meaning around like a pretzel. Prove it to yourself in this exercise:

- Imagine your boss saying this sentence *without expressing any emotion.* "I just spoke with Doug, and he told me that report came from your department." What does it mean? First, you and your boss both know someone named Doug. Doug identified that some particular report you both know about came from the department where you work. Nothing but information. Let's bend it with emotion.

- *What if your boss said it happily:* "I just spoke with Doug, and he told me that report came from your department!" Now what does it mean? It sounds like praise. This report is something of which you can be proud.
- *What if your boss said it sadly:* "I just spoke with Doug, and he told me that report came from your department." Now this can mean it's a disappointment, or maybe an embarrassment. Hmmm.
- *What if your boss said it angrily:* "I just spoke with Doug, and he told me that report came from your department." Now it means you're in trouble. You crossed your boss or did something wrong. Uh-oh.

How can one sentence mean four different things without changing any of the words? Simple. *Emotion, or lack of it, is a huge part of the meaningful content of any message.* On a piano, the same notes can be played simply, in a straightforward way, with peppy brightness, pounding fury or mournful sorrow, just as your words can be played different ways by your feelings to mean different things.

Happy, sad, mad and neutral all play a role in what the words mean. How can we as speakers and communicators even consider ignoring the power of emotions? But so many business professionals work hard to achieve a perpetual calm, to lock themselves permanently in a neutral state, to insulate themselves from feeling or receiving emotions at their place of business. The idea of neutral permanence, especially as a supposed standard for professionalism, is a fundamental misunderstanding responsible for a lack of emotional intelligence, sensitivity and persuasive potential in the workplace. For the sake of emotional comfort and security, authenticity, peak performance and contribution are sacrificed—particularly within the population of professional women.

Emotion is fundamental to human communication. It is content in and of itself. If you don't believe me, the next time you make a mistake and upset someone you love, try apologizing without actually feeling any regret. That person probably will be hurt, and you'll have to apologize again.

Since you'll probably be frustrated about having to apologize twice, express a little anger with your second apology. Now that person will become more upset, and you'll have to apologize a third time.

By your third apology, your relationship is hanging on a thread, so why not try feeling regretful (a variation on sad) when you apologize—and you won't have to apologize a fourth time.

Get it right the first time. Consider choosing the most effective emotional strategy at the same time that you're thinking of the right words to say. This is always be best for both of you. Try bending the words with emotion to create a win-win that brings you forward together. Choosing effective feelings is a proactive strategy that is as valid as choosing effective words.

■ Emotions Manage Body Language

Bite your tongue and you can hold back words but nothing will stop your body language from speaking volumes about what you are feeling. Emotion's communicative power is visible to anyone around you, *when you talk—and when you don't.*

Picture someone sitting in a chair, doing and saying nothing. What will you conclude? Likely it will depend upon the emotions they are feeling while they sit. They might seem happy, sad, mad, or indifferent, based on the thoughts they're thinking, the emotions created by the thoughts and the subtle body language display resulting from their feelings.

You don't have to be doing anything in order for your body language to be communicating. Whatever you are or are not doing, your feelings show through the subtleties of any combination of expression, gesture, posture or voice tone. Emotion is the source of nonverbal communication.

Emotion is to body language what thoughts are to words. Words don't inherently contain any meaning. Meaning is in the mind, and the mind symbolically delivers the meaning that it perceives to other people through words. Similarly, body language doesn't inherently contain any emotion.

Emotion is in the heart and heart delivers emotion to other people symbolically through body language.

Every moment, you are delivering nonverbal signals, representing a near-constant flow of intended or unintended nonverbal messages. Participation and self-awareness are fundamental to managing the unspoken language that never stops speaking.

If you want to control your body language,
you have to focus on your feelings.

Screen actors practice feeling different feelings so when they need to display a certain flavor of presence they can choose the one that triggers the desired body language for the scene. That's acting.

The same is true for presenters. The *last* thing audiences want is "play acting." Everyone wants authenticity, so work on authentic emotions, and let your authentic emotions run the nonverbals. Don't mask fear, or hide behind a phony smile. Forced or faked emotion is you staying safely in the cage while sending your body language out to represent you. People can see through that as easily as you can see a fake cry on a bad sitcom. If you can feel it, the audience will believe it, because they'll know first-hand that you are present. First, use appreciation to neutralize fear and form a connection. Next, feel the feelings that match your message. That way you respectfully create a safe environment, and inspire audiences within it.

*Focusing on your feelings is the best way
we know to control body language.*

This is a very straighforward idea, but it takes practice to reliably deploy. Fortunately, life gives you many chances to practice feeling. Choose a feeling, right now, either happy, sad or mad. See if you can feel it. If you can't, try again later. You'll probably get there by thinking of different thoughts, memories and ideas that trigger emotions.

You can also attempt emotions in different environments with other people present. Feel a certain way, and watch to see if it impacts the behavior of those around you. Be smart about how and when you experiment in this way. Think constructively and consider it a playground for participating in your authenticity, as opposed to a trick to manipulate people.

■ Emotions Influence the Tone of Interactions

Recently I was coaching a group of people who were preparing for an important sales pitch and everyone was under pressure. The team leader was steaming mad at a key presenter who hadn't done his homework on this important project. The tension between these two was palpable, impacting everyone. The leader relentlessly slipped biting inuendo into the advice he was giving to the underprepared employee, who kept making light of the scolding remarks. This caused the leader to bite harder, and the underprepared man to become more dismissive of the hardly disguised accusations about his work ethic. It was too subtle to call them on it, but it was too antagonistic to overlook, and everyone was on edge as a result. I decided that this would be a constructive opportunity to practice influencing the tone of the environment with my emotions.

I elected a very positive, yet assertive feeling, and I decided to stick with it no matter what happened. This was a compound emotion—all at once stern (which is a touch of anger), and optimistic (which is a dose of happy in anticipation of the possible outcomes). While the rest of the team members were visibly acting out a state of calm to avoid drawing attention to themselves, I remained vulnerably visible, beaming my serious, positive, "bring-it-on" emotion like a wood-burning stove in a cold room.

First I noticed how my emotional commitment affected my body language. Without even trying, I found myself speaking slower and with more certainty. My tone was leaderly, carrying more authority. I sounded like someone who believed in the team sitting around the table. Soon I noticed changes in the innocent bystanders in the room. Where before they were forcing a false neutral, their cage doors were starting to open and their stress over their boss' approach was becoming visible.

As I continued to radiate an unwavering "we can do this thing" vibe, their defensiveness and fear was starting to fade, and they began inching out of their hiding places. I started to see little expressions of passion and confidence. Before my eyes, the team's body language was transforming, from the vacant stare of a ninth-grade social studies class getting scolded by its teacher, to something more like a team of passionate, confident professionals. They were believing in my emotions, unconsciously anchoring their self-perceptions on my energy instead of that of their boss.

As I noticed this, I began verbally affirming people for what they were doing right. I affirmed the expertise and knowledge of the underprepared team member, believing in him at any level of preparedness. And I affirmed the team leader for his simple expectation that everybody needs to be up to speed on the project details. I was reinforcing both sides of the fence with affirming emotional confidence which confirmed everything on the table, *and made it okay* at the same time.

The chemistry between the two adversaries gradually shifted away from the combative energy they had and toward a constructive energy focused on the task at hand because I'd removed the emotional table they had been on the opposite sides of. They became a team again because I changed the chemistry of the room by relentlessly pouring my serious, confident optimism into the goup-wide petri dish where emotions mixed. Without changing the content of the discussion, *I led them with presence* to the positive work tone they needed in order to work together. We went into the interview as a team, and won the multi-million dollar project.

You can practice emotions in many situations to see how they impact you and the world. Everyday there are squabbles to disrupt, losses to empathize with, routines to bring excitement to, awkward silences to refresh and flat moments to invigorate. Notice and identify feelings that come on their own. If a feeling is fading, see if you can extend it longer than it would normally have lasted. When you are experiencing a feeling at a low level, see if you can intensify it. Can you choose a different feeling than the one you have right now, and trigger it out of the blue?

Tone is a big part of any reliable win-win presenting strategy, and hundreds of situations you face every day provide opportunities to practice, learn and master the language that never stops talking through your body. Family and friends provide many great opportunities to practice emotions. I recommend you experiment when you're involved in relatively insignificant situations.

Is Emotional Leveraging Manipulative?

This is a common question we hear, and we totally understand it because people don't want to be manipulative. When you manipulate people, it's dishonest or covert in some way and you're influencing them without letting them know that you're intending to do so.

Intentionally choosing your emotions can raise this question because the nonverbal language that communicates feelings seems to be less direct or overt than the verbal language that communicates thoughts.

If you're truthful and authentic regarding the emotions you choose, and you really feel them genuinely in the moment, emotional leveraging is no more manipulative than carefully choosing your words. Ethically, you should mean what you say, and also what you feel.

Imagine a situation where you're facing a scary-cool opportunity. This is something you want, and believe that you can do well. So you *are* confident, but also nervous about it because this is the moment of *selling* yourself to secure the opportunity.

You have two authentic options when facing an emotional crossroads:

1. You could be a stammering wreck because you are genuinely nervous.
2. You could be a passionate and confident professional because this is an opportunity you genuinely want and you believe in yourself.

Both reactions are genuine, but one seems clearly better, and it requires emotional leveraging to achieve. If you go with the flow of your own anxiety, that would be true, and it would make the decider's job easier by weeding you out of the running. If you *manually trigger* your passion and confidence, that would be both authentic and *useful*, because you would be showcasing your strengths to the decision-maker under pressure. But you have to consciously choose your emotions to get to authenticity.

It's important to build your ability to be emotionally intentional. If you practice choosing the right emotions as much as you practice choosing the right words, you would have a much improved chance of displaying the right body language to help you achieve your goals.

Convinced yet? Could emotional leveraging really be ethical? It's your future on the line, so it has to be your call. When it's my future, I consider it too risky to leave emotions to chance and run the risk of a massive miscommunication. I dread having my fear color me as hesitant and unsure. That's a completely inaccurate picture of me, and I've been burned by that kind of miscommunication before. Displaying my passion portrays me more accurately and provides a *more* authentic representation of how I would be if I got the opportunity, than does a display of situational nerves caused by the pressures of selling myself.

> *Manipulating emotions isn't manipulative*
> *as long as your goal is to bring out your authenticity.*

Working with Emotions

Professionals need to understand the important functions of emotions as they maximize, emphasize, inspire, convince and authenticate.

If I created the impression that emotions are pretty complex, read on. The next step is learning how to simplify the process of using them, making emotional participation practical for communication.

A Color Wheel for Emotion

In art class, you learn that three colors make up one basic color wheel. You can make any color by combining red, blue and yellow. I wish we had a similar tool to work with emotions. Instead, we have hundreds of words for feelings, ranging from furious to euphoric to anguish.

Filmmaker Rob Nilsson used a simple approach to emotions. He recognized only three basic emotions: joy, rage and despair, and achieved all the other emotions by working with the main three.

When Pete and I entered the corporate arena, the idea of using acting skills for real business challenges was met with some pushback. Business professionals didn't like the idea of faking anything. Neither did we.

Our goal with any screen actor was to find a place of authenticity. The parallel we drew between actors and business professionals was that neither consistently had the correct emotional energy to match their truthful passion or conviction. If presentation pressure triggered fear and self-doubt, we believed it was more authentic to actively create the emotion that more truthfully represented the speaker and the message. Our goal was a new form of honesty, where people shared more and were committed to finding the emotional state that best captured their truth.

So SagePresence adapted Nilsson's three emotions to the less dramatic happy, sad, mad and put them into our "Color Wheel of Emotion" as a model for working with feelings. Occasionally we mix emotions, but mostly we work the primaries.

Happy, sad, and mad are broad-stroke, primary emotions and the rest of the emotions are variations.

- *Thrilled* would fall inside of happy.
- *Depressed* would fall inside of sad.
- *Annoyed* would fall inside of mad.

All emotions fall within the big three. At SagePresence we stick to these primaries, largely working on varying the degree or level we feel and display.

Like actors, a great presenter needs to feel *happy* at the right times, *sad* at the right times and *mad* at the right times—and in different amounts, depending on what the scenario calls for. When presenters do this, their audience will feel their message. So how do you pick correctly?

When and How Much Emotion to Use

What is the right emotion, and when is the right time? What is the right amount? These questions have a clear answer:

All you have to do is feel the words you're saying
and your feelings will adjust accordingly.

If you're talking about a loss, sad will come naturally. If it's a loved one, the feeling will be stronger than if it's a project that went to a competitor. If you're celebrating a success, then happy should kick in. If you're saying something serious, then some level of sternness, a low-level of mad is going to creep in.

If you practice feeling your words, you'll find that the right emotions in the right degree appear automatically.

The Good, the Bad and the Ugly—the Constructive and Destructive Uses for Emotions

I used to think emotions were either good or bad. I thought happy was the only good one, and sad and mad were bad. This was a bleak outlook, where life was proportionally more negative than positive. But this was incorrect thinking. Emotions aren't stacked against you. All feelings can be good or bad, depending on the context. I was just looking at the equation all wrong.

Have you ever had a time when you were feeling nothing in particular, and you heard a song that made you feel melancholy? Melancholy is a negative experience, but suddenly you found yourself downloading the song from iTunes and playing it again because you didn't want the feeling to go away. Could this 'bad feeling' be good in some way?

Emotions are not to be feared, but pursued. They are more than simple reactions to tell you whether your current situation is bad or good. Instead, feelings are an integral part of experiencing and navigating life.

In a real-life context, sad or mad may seem to be a horrible experience, but when actors feel sad in an acting class, they say it is fun!

What that tells me as a director is that negative emotions aren't like pain. The vast majority of pain experiences are reliably negative. Pain hurts. But sad doesn't necessarily hurt. Mad isn't necessarily a negative experience.

Out of context, negative emotions can feel amazing.

Sad feels kind of good in the tear-jerking movie you paid for, knowing it would make you cry. And mad can be fun in a friendly political debate with a couple of hotheads and a pitcher of beer. So positive and negative emotions are more context-sensitive than physical pain.

Understanding this changed my relationship with sad and mad. What you need to grasp in order to use them positively is an easy-to-understand concept:

Emotion can be used to build up or tear down.

So what makes an emotion constructive or destructive? Establishing concrete guidelines is tricky because emotions are more subject to interpretation than words. They are nonverbal but they are always talking through body language. They are continually experienced but are less on the radar of the average person, leaving considerable room for messages and interpretations outside of conscious awareness.

I've witnessed business professionals get away with damaging emotional messages in the workplace because the hurtful content was merely implied as innuendo communicated through their feelings. It can be hard for the recipient of an emotional attack to call their boss or coworker on something that was never explicitly said, even though the implications were viscerally experienced.

I've also seen positive emotional messages go unnoticed, which can be just as unfortunate. Have you ever experienced a boss seeming pleased with your performance, but leaving you to wonder why they didn't directly confirm their satisfaction in words?

The constructiveness or destructiveness of emotions depends a lot on how the verbal and nonverbal components of communication play off each other. Speaking constructive words to match constructive emotions is like pairing wine with food—each changes the other when used together.

The better you understand emotional functionality, particularly in business, the more you'll be able to pair your emotions with your words to communicate your truth.

- Let's start with **happy.** The celebration of a job well done, or providing praise to affirm and encourage desirable behavior would be a good use for happy at work. But Happy can be destructive, too. Laughing at a colleague's failure or celebrating a competitor's defeat is very different from celebrating your own victory, even though the emotion is the same. Have you ever, perhaps secretly, waited for someone you don't like to screw up and when they finally did, you enjoyed their failure, or maybe even gushed about it to a friend? This is a destructive use of happy.

- How about **sad**? Sad can shut people down or spoil momentum, slowing motivation to a halt, stunting productivity for an individual or deflating initiative throughout a team. That's destructive. But sad *can be incredibly constructive* when you're talking about empathy.

    Here's an example:

    Years ago, as the owner of a company, I had to fire a woman. It was a small entrepreneurial startup with no human relations department, and it hadn't yet matured to the point of having any sort of termination guidelines. I hated firing this woman, but I had to, and when I did, I felt her pain and she could see that I cared. Because she experienced my care and respect for her in that difficult time, she felt positive about the company even after being released. Months later, she felt comfortable referring us to a company she went to work for, which eventually brought us business.

It happened that on the same day I was to release this woman, another director was releasing someone from his department. In that office, where the other employee was fired that same day, the deed was carried out without empathy, and that spiraled into a wrongful termination suit.
This helped me put a dollar value on taking the time to feel someone's pain—a constructive and profitable use of sad.
Sad is also a key ingredient for building trust and intimacy between speakers and audiences.

As a presenter, I openly share sadness as I talk about struggle, loss, or failure, and my audiences have an experience of being confided in. My actions clearly imply that there is a trust between us, and the intimate act of confiding leads them to trust me and to be trustworthy in return. By confiding in my audience, I create a safe environment for authenticity and people treat me as though they know me intimately, even though we may be seeing each other for the first time.

- **Mad** is a powerful emotion that gets a bad rap because it's so clearly tied to destruction and to people getting hurt. But mad can also be extremely constructive if used to drive people forward toward places they want to go, or that are good for them. Using mad when you present can be very effective in guiding an audience to take what you are saying seriously. You don't have to be angry at anyone, but the careful use of anger intensifies words, and communicates seriousness. Prove it to yourself. Feel neutral then say out loud, "This will change your life." Next, say it with anger, a word at a time, very slowly and loudly. Now reel it in, bringing the volume to a more normal level and use a seething yet quiet anger to make your tone stern and serious. You'll notice that it doesn't sound mean or mad. It should sound positive and constructive, and very important.

In your presentations, use mad to drive people forward, motivate action and communicate seriousness. It's true that road rage, violence, intimidation and humiliation are also products of mad. People fly off the handle, cut people down verbally, and put others in their place with mad. Because of its obvious damaging effects, mad can be a slippery slope toward destruction. Use it only constructively to drive people upward, toward good places and never to hurt anyone with it.

Avoid pointing anger too directly at any one person. I use it in front of people, but not at them. That means, I don't linger too long on any single person with my eye contact when I have a very serious tone. That way I don't appear to be scolding anyone. The use of mad I'm talking about will accompany positive subject matter, like encouraging others to achieve an important objective, or rise to seize an opportunity. These sorts of subjects have power when impassioned with anger, and are unlikely to be misread as chewing someone out. Pay attention to the audience to ensure you are reading their reaction correctly.

Permission to Feel Freely

Most professionals we talk with are intentionally trying to keep their emotions inside a cage. I'm here to give you permission to use your emotions constructively throughout your work day. Consider letting them out, actively choosing your feelings and strictly committing to being constructive. The more you practice using emotions in constructive ways, the more control you will develop, including the ability to dial your emotions down when appropriate. *Emotional mastery* can occur if you *feel* your emotions frequently and intentionally, while adhering to the constructive uses that build the people around you.

> ***Working your emotional controls***
> ***helps you turn them on—and turn them off.***

Making Emotions Safe

The *appreciation sandwich* is the best tool I know to ensure that "negative" emotions land constructively without hurting anyone. Appreciation, as we've established, builds a connection of instant trust and caring with another person. Inside of that connection, you can share emotions comfortably. Appreciation before and after a "negative" emotion, such as sad or mad, makes the expression okay, and makes it appropriate for work.

Appreciation sandwiching is a close cousin to another version of sandwiching we hear about in business, relating to constructive criticism. If you sandwich a statement of criticism between two affirmations, the recipient doesn't experience it as a verbal slap in the face.

Appreciation sandwiching does that for any sensitive emotion, protecting the listener with a safe respectfulness on both ends of the negative or sensitive emotion. SagePresence and its clients have successfully leveraged very delicate or extra stern emotions inside of corporate environments because of the appreciation at both ends. Appreciation extends a feeling of safety from inside you out into the interactive space. In that way we can bring our safety with us and extend it to everyone around us.

I've expressed more emotion than anyone I know in business settings, without suffering negative consequences. I would boldly suggest that this technique makes almost any emotion appropriate in nearly any setting. Take it slow, and pay attention to how your words land with your audience. In the end, you will be praised for your authenticity and daring transparency, even in places where emotion has been deemed risky.

Appreciate first.
Then feel whatever emotion the message calls for.
End with appreciation, so the message leaves your audience feeling
cared for and respected.

This is appreciation sandwiching. Do it, and it will free you to fly the authentic skies, genuinely and respectfully.

Emotional Venting

The intentional use of authentic, constructive feelings will also help you vent so you can avoid emotional buildup. If you're regularly inspiring others, showing empathy, celebrating progress and driving serious matters forward, your emotions won't bottle up.

Emotional buildup is what leads to explosive rage, or crumpling into tears. People who experience this tend to find emotions too risky and try to turn them off. Emotional pressure builds up internally while on the outside the person appears emotionless.

They pay the price for bottling their emotions with:
- A reduction in their potential to influence
- Numbness to the experiences of the world around them

- Any number of health problems related to stress, including fatigue, ulcers and even cancer
- The explosion that results from the built-up pressure which can lead to damaging both reputations and relationship.

Expressing emotions isn't just a means for avoiding all of this negative fallout, it's a tool to steer your career into positive territory, building your reputation and enhancing your relationships.

Emotions and Professional Women

Jane worked in a total man's world at an industrial plant. She was a mid-range executive, going nowhere fast. People didn't like her and political rivalries existed, particularly with the few other women in the plant. She tried her hardest to be what she thought the men were like, but she had been passed up for promotion and didn't know how to move forward in her career.

We were sad when Jane told us, "Every day I take off my real self and hang it in the closet at home and go to work as an empty shell. I have lived my entire career that way because the real person is filled with passion and emotion, and there's no place for any of that here."

Jane believed that there was no room for authenticity in her workplace. Her leadership was occasionally understated, and often cold and heartless. If she didn't like something or someone, her icy glare could deliberately intimidate. That was how she produced results, and how she led.

Using exactly what she had been leaving behind, we showed her something new. Taking the most familiar part of her—her passion—we showed her how it fit into the workplace. Exploring the useful functions of happy, sad and mad, we identified where they could be constructive and prescribed authenticity as her salvation.

We had her improvise the feeling of the three core emotions, and she:

- suddenly saw how sad allowed her to empathize; she wanted to empathize, desperately
- practiced using happy to affirm and celebrate—something she had always hoped to do at work and wished others would do for her
- learned where mad could be constructive in showing seriousness and commitment and in driving people forward toward a win-win scenario; she had no idea that mad could ever be constructive.

All of this was new, yet familiar. She wasn't experiencing something completely alien—this was the way she was at home, and in the rest of her life. But for the first time she was at work, having feelings.

Suddenly she stopped talking, dropped her head into her hands, and wept. I was worried that I broke something, but I gave her some space for whatever she was going through. Finally, I asked if she was okay, and she came up from her hands. Tears were in her eyes, but she was smiling.

She choked out that she was okay. More than okay. "You just gave me permission to bring myself to work. I didn't ever stop to think that maybe there was room for me here. But now I know there is, and I just made an oath to myself never again to leave my authentic self behind."

Earlier we had filmed Jane in her shell, as she was at work, and we showed her that. One of the greatest delights of my career was to show her the 'after' video and introduce her to the new Jane so she could see herself alive, authentic and amazing.

Jane received two promotions that year and completely changed her leadership style, based on her genuine personality. She quit trying to be what she *thought* the men wanted. Her bosses were thrilled, and clearly had never wanted her to be anything other than herself.

Jane discovered that work could be a place
for passion, seriousness, celebration and success.

Emotional Intentionality—The Method

Think of a joystick—it's not like an on-off switch. Instead, it pushes *toward* something. If you put a joystick on the Emotional Color Wheel, you could push it toward *Happy, Sad* or *Mad* to experience more of that feeling. If you want less of one emotion that isn't serving you, you could push toward a different one that you do want.

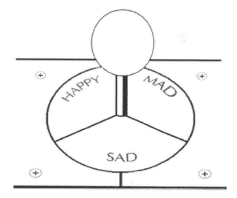

Neutral is in the middle, and this is also a legitimate place to be. Maybe you meditate, which is the practice of finding this neutral place.

I want to give you a means to reduce unwanted emotions that does not require a meditative time-out.

Practice *picking a different emotion* as a means to exit from an emotion you don't want. In this approach, your attention isn't on turning off an emotion, but turning one on. And because each emotion has its constructive uses, happy, sad and mad will all be viable choices. When you practice turning any one of them on, you will create a means to turn off either of the other two.

Emotions are triggered by thoughts. You change your feelings by adjusting your thoughts. Practice conjuring up specific thoughts and memories, then let your feelings morph with them.

Change your thoughts
in order to change your emotions
so that you can change your body language.

Your goal is not constant emotional control; it's momentary control. Emotion is an automatic process, and this is how it should be. What you want is to be able to take it out of automatic, and put it into manual at certain times. These might be during a presentation or important conversation—when you want to feel a specific way to ensure that your body language says what you want it to say.

With some practice of intentionally pushing toward the emotions of happy, sad and mad during unimportant moments, you will be able to consciously change your emotions when your automatic feeling isn't helping you.

The classic situation is when you need to display confidence—but can't. Thoughts of doubt and uncertainty trigger a worrisome sinking feeling which is a variation of sad. Your first instinct will be to want to reduce that sad feeling. But this will lead you to an emotional flatline. Instead, I recommend you choose either happy or mad because both can help you display confidence.

Happy is a great way to show confidence. Through your joy, the audience can experience your passion. Joy communicates that you see opportunity. People who have passion and see opportunity look confident.

Mad works fantastically well to show confidence too. Anger is the emotional energy of seriousness and commitment, and it shows drive. People who have seriousness and drive look very confident.

When I find myself suffering from a momentary drop in confidence, which happens regularly, I will choose happy or mad, based on whichever one I feel closer to at the time. This restarts my authentic confidence. Either way, I won't try to reduce my sadness or numb the sinking feeling; it will go away as a result of choosing one of the other two.

It takes practice to do this, but once you get it down, you'll be able to consistently rely on this process to spontaneously produce the emotions you need to win your audience over.

I don't see jump-starting my confidence as faking anything. I really am confident—it's momentary fear that knocks me into an inauthentic state and once I'm back in my authentic state, my automatic emotions are fine again.

You can mostly trust your emotions to flow the way they should. Your goal is to develop the ability to "go to manual" for short periods of time, putting yourself in the desired emotional state. Once you're in your zone, you can continue on automatic again.

Feeling what you want is much easier than trying to "unfeel" the feeling you don't want. Practice moving toward emotions so that you can choose the emotion you want in the moments when they are most important.

Mixing Emotions

Painters mix primary colors to create all the shades they need. When I was in art school, I didn't just stick to the primaries. Without mixing, I'd have had no orange, purple, brown or the more subtle hues like auburn or violet.

Emotional primaries also mix together to make different emotions. Beyond the primaries, you'll also have blissful, exultant, melancholy, heart- broken, livid, annoyed and hundreds more. All emotions are created from the primaries—some combination and degree of happy, sad and mad.

But you'll be relieved to hear that you don't have to worry about mixing emotions. You could spend a lifetime learning to master what you already do automatically. If you commit to feeling your words as you say them, all those nuances will simply be there for you. All you have to do is focus on the primaries when you practice, and in the moment of your real presentations, feel your words.

So I let emotions mix organically, and I don't practice creating emotional cocktails. Except for one.

The "Happy/Mad Cocktail"

Imagine if you could:

- Cue up winning presence as you were closing a sale
- Recover your confidence after being thrown off-guard in a crucial meeting
- Bring conviction to the moments you feel the most uncertain

With some practice, you can do all this and more. The "how" involves the only mix of emotions I specifically practice. I call it the "Happy/Mad Cocktail" —a powerfully positive flavor of assertiveness that comes when you feel *happy* and *mad* at the same time.

Does Happy/Mad sound like a contradiction? It's not. As it turns out, Happy and mad mix well, like yellow and red mix to make orange. When

I want to really move an audience forward with inspiring confidence, I do it with the Happy/Mad Cocktail. Happy shows the confidence of passion and opportunity. Mad shows the confidence of seriousness and drive. Together they show you as someone who sees the opportunity and has the conviction to get there. No emotional energy communicates more confidence than these two do when they're mixed together.

Politicians use this technique all the time when they rally their voters for a big election. Sports coaches use it to rev up their team before a big game. "Okay, let's get out there, and teach them what it means to play to win!"

This technique is used all the time in business. When you want to inspire action, or when you strongly believe something, you tend to feel both a little happy (about opportunity) and a little angry (about the prospects of failure), and with that energy, you can urge others to take a step.

Imagine this sentence, first with no emotion at all. Try saying it out loud, as only information—just the facts. "This is a big opportunity. We have no choice but to jump all over this."

Next, read it out loud again, and this time say it happily. "This is a Big Opportunity! We have No Choice but to Jump All Over this!" Did you feel and hear a positive "Yippee!" accompanying the words? If you did, so would others, and that would be motivating.

Now grit your teeth, furl your eyebrows and say the same sentence with a no-kidding, intensity of anger. *"This is a big opportunity. We*

have no choice but to jump all over this." That should work too, in a very different, urgent way. When I tried it, I noticed that I slowed down and really hit it hard. It sounded strong.

Now try the Happy/Mad Cocktail. Say that same sentence with *both happy* and *mad* at the same time. Try to hear the joy of opportunity and the serious "push" of anger.*"This is a Big Opportunity! We have No Choice but to Jump All Over this!"*

Could you do it? It should sound like a battle cry that sings with opportunity. It has the "bring-it-on" vibe, with the irresistible draw of anticipation. Practice it, in rehearsal and in the not-so-important moments, so you can test and confirm for yourself that this Happy/Mad Cocktail can be authentic and influential. If you're still confused about what I'm talking about, watch a sports movie and pay attention to the coach.

Happy and mad together create a driving excitement—
the taste of the victory.

Emotions During Presentations

After establishing a connection using appreciation, emotions should change during a presentation or conversation. Different parts will be happy, sad and mad and will feature the 'win energy' of the Happy/ Mad Cocktail. Feelings accompany words, and if they don't, your body language will be flat. And flat (in small doses) is fine too—being occasionally neutral to punctuate and create more contrast between information and inspiration.

Emotions and Rehearsal

When you rehearse your presentation, practice at least one run-through with the focus on *feeling your words.* This is an open-ended drill, because you can't ensure any particular emotional result. Make a commitment to being open and in the moment regarding your feelings.

Ask yourself, "Can I open myself up to feeling my words?" and do your practice run. The words themselves will decide what you should feel because you gave yourself permission to feel them. The drill is very much about the permission—more about *allowing* than *forcing*.

When I'm standing in the wings, waiting for my presentation to start, I'll repeat my invitation to feel: "Dean, can you open yourself up to feel your words?" This is my commitment to *mean* what I say when I take the stage.

Like a golfer with the muscle memory of a good swing, you need to build your heart's muscle memory of tolerating vulnerability and allowing feelings to flow through you. Feeling is the most important 'swing' that you have as a speaker, and 'felt words' will dramatically increase your chances of hitting an accurate long drive, if not a hole in one, with your audience.

Chemistry Summary

What you start with connection blossoms into *chemistry*. Appreciation is the setup, and *emotion* is the payoff. You want the connection so that you can create an intimate conversational experience, and you want conversational intimacy so you can have chemistry.

Chemistry is the mixture of your emotions and their emotions and the way they mix affects everyone involved.

Sharing emotions is an act of confiding in a person or an audience. It implies that a trusting relationship already exists and as a result, usually creates one.

Working with emotions, and feeling them inside your presentations, is how you inspire.

- Embrace them, stick to their constructive uses and sandwich them with appreciation to make them comfortable and safe
- Practice turning on the primaries of happy, sad and mad instead of wasting time trying to turn off emotions you don't want
- Trust that feelings will brilliantly manage your body language and open you up to feeling what you say

Feel your words as you speak them and you will create chemistry between you and your audience.

Chapter 5

Compelling Messages

LEWIS: Everything's a story, kid. Stories are what help us make sense of the world.

*Script from the movie
"The Lookout"*

The pursuit of 'magic words' is one of the most flawed quests since the Holy Grail. Perfect words are like a grand mirage. You perceive them on the horizon, yet as you near them, the magic disappears.

Sometimes, the right words fall out of your mouth like a happy accident, and someone says, "Perfect! Say that again so I can write it down," and you're completely unable to repeat your own eloquence. Or, you fantasize the perfect exchange: "I'll say this, and she'll say that." But when the moment arrives, it doesn't happen at all the way you imagined. You fumble, wishing you could find the right thing to say, but it's not coming.

Why is it that:

1. Some people always seem to find the power of words when you can't?
2. We face silver-tongued devils who wield words like swords, and against them we're defenseless?
3. The words of others charm and entrance, while yours bore?
4. We have access to some really good words? And we recognize

the way they string together occasionally makes them ring like poetry. I sometimes use poetic combinations of words without even trying. When it happens, I rather enjoy it. But poetry is not mission-critical. I stake no claims in my language, because I don't think that words are as important as the intent that drives them.

So you can relax and give up the search, because *no magic words exist.* No expertly crafted message could ever outperform your average or even clumsy phrases, delivered from the heart with passion and conviction. You can breathe magic into words through a powerful delivery, but there is a more reliable path to eloquence, and it's found in the spaces between words and the thoughts that inspired them.

> *Magnificence is less in the words*
> *and more in the way they are strung together.*

Words exist to share thoughts. Your messages are attempts to articulate what's in your mind, so someone else can understand your ideas similarly to the way you do.

Messages have content. They *mean* something, and if your messages say to your audience what you want them to say, you are achieving communication that's absolutely priceless. To do this, you need to think like an engineer who blueprints and troubleshoots the structural integrity of a communicated thought.

Don't think so much about the specific words coming out of your mouth. Focus on the *structure* of your message. Structure is systematic and reliable, and from it *meaningful* words will flow. If structure is right, you'll find hundreds of ways to tackle the words—and it will still say the same thing. We've found a specific structure that brings reliable elegance with relative ease. With it, average words can have a magically influential effect because they *take people somewhere.*

The structure I'm talking about is story. Story, which has been with us since the dawn of humankind, is the basis of all communication. Early people saw the sequential relationship between past, present and future and needed a way to share the meanings they perceived. Words became the symbols to express the meaning in the mind—what happened yesterday, what's happening right now outside of our direct view and what will happen tomorrow.

Business communication can also use story, although it seldom begins with "once upon a time." When your business messages are formatted in the movements of story, they make more sense, have more flow, generate more influence and withstand being retold repeatedly without distortion.

If you tell a story to one person, and he or she tells it to another who retells it to yet another, the words will undoubtedly change each time. But the story-structured message holds up far longer than an unstructured message. Why? Because structural integrity preserves the intent of your general meaning, and leaves room for interpretation and variations in the wording.

Message Structure Made Simple

The SagePresence process of developing messages began in 2001, when we applied the structure of a Hollywood screenplay to sales presentations. Our thinking was that the movie business had mastered keeping people on the edge of their seats in the dark for two hours, even at the end of a long day, after a heavy dinner and beer. Therefore, we assumed that an adaptation of Hollywood's screenplay structure could help us captivate corporate audiences.

Even though our first attempt involved too many steps, the approach helped our client win their way into a $45 million project. The process worked, but it was far too complex to be practical, and it would never be a useful process in conversation.

Because we wanted a method that would work quickly, with or without any prep time, we spent the next decade refining and distilling it. When we were done, our fifteen-step process had only four components, and worked in any situation. The result was one tool to navigate any version of communication you may be facing.

The Four Parts of a Story

Three of the four story components are so obvious you barely think about them. Can you identify the big three? Take a moment to think of your answer.

You probably guessed right, because it's that easy. The four key parts of any story are:

1. Beginning
2. Middle
3. End
4. Main Character

The first three are basically all you have to know to structure powerful messages, as long as you grasp their function. And main character is getting the *who* of the story right, ensuring that your listeners care about your message. Let's set main character aside for a moment and study beginning, middle and end.

Two Situations That Describe a Change

Beginning describes a situation. Nothing happens in the beginning of a story. Ending captures a different situation, and in fact, nothing is really happening in the end of a story either. But the two situations are not the same so together they describe a change.

You mostly notice only things that change in your life and tend to ignore things that remain the same. That's why you take things for granted, and as the saying goes, "You never know what you've got until it's gone." What changes, registers. Animals are wired to recognize change and ignore everything else, and many species will not see a predator right in front of them unless it's moving.

Messages that don't describe a change don't have a meaningful point. The situations at the beginning and end have to be different in order for meaning to register at all. If they are the same, no change has occurred and therefore no story has been communicated.

A message says *nothing* if it begins with a company doing really well, and ends with it still doing well. However, if you talk about a struggling business that comes to thrive, you communicate a meaningful story. Or you could tell a story about a business that last year was reasonably profitable, and is now extraordinarily so.

Stories describe a change, so one of the first questions I ask when I am designing a message is: *What change am I describing?*

The second question is: *How extreme can I make the change?* The wider the range, the bigger the impact. As a filmmaker, I know that people respond more positively to a powerless peasant becoming a powerful leader than they would an already influential leader gaining even more influence.

The bigger the change, the more powerful the story.

Action Is in the Middle

Beginnings and endings are situations, and everything that happens in a story is in the middle. The action causes the change. Here's an example of a complete story we created with a client who was preparing a presentation to his boss. This example distinguishes each of the three basic components to show a beginning **(B-)** situation changing into an ending **(E+)** situation because of a middle **(M)** action:

B- Customers were complaining about excessive wait times for technical support.

M We created and publicized a user-friendly online tutorial addressing many of the most frequently asked questions.

E+ User complaints are now down over 50 percent.

One situation changes into another because of an action. If your presentation begins with your company losing ground to your competitors today and ends with the company as a market leader in six months, the action in the middle will probably be your *plan to get there.*

If you stay true to this formula, every message you structure will communicate a clear, complete and compelling idea.

Everyone Loves a Happy Ending

Take a moment and think about traditional stories. Most begin with a problem and end with that problem resolved. If a character is sad at the beginning, she'll probably be happy at the end. Commonly, change tends to go from negative to positive—not so happy to happy.

Human beings are climbers and we are driven by our own insatiable need to get from where we are now to the next higher elevation. People feed off the feeling that things are getting better. So in business, when we are exposed to messages that make us feel things are improving, or that promise to take us to a better place in the future, we'll be motivated to listen.

Therefore, beginnings need to communicate not-so-happy situations and endings need to communicate happier ones—the greater the change, the better.

Tragedies Have Their Place

Not all stories go from negative to positive. Some stories end up in a place worse than where they started. Positive-to-negative stories are happy beginnings that end up not so happy. They provide a warning, or cautionary tale.

A positive-to-negative story is a great wake-up call, like a splash of cold water, to set the stage for something serious. It warns you how bad your situation is right now, or how bad it could get. It speaks *against* actions, instead of *for* them. Negative messages tend to motivate you by scaring you, as they take you from a happy beginning situation **(B+)** to a not-so-happy ending situation **(E-).**

B+ Smith-Corona was a market leader in typewriters.

M But they didn't change with the times.

E- So they went out of business.

This is a cautionary tale, warning you about what happens if you don't change with the times. It starts with a good situation (leading the market), has an action in the middle (standing still), and a bad ending situation (out of business). If you were trying to send someone a wake-up call and force them to see that they need to change, you might choose to tell a positive-to-negative story like this.

Delivering bad news is another example of a positive-to-negative story.

B+ We were confident we had a good plan.

M We did exactly what we said we would do,
but it wasn't enough.

E- We didn't hit our numbers.

This is important information. Your company failed, but at least there was a plan and it was followed. It's not very uplifting, but people need to understand, and sometimes you have to tell these kind of stories.

When you use positive-to-negative stories, don't leave your audience there. Leverage the unhappy ending to motivate new action. Use it for a new story that begins with this unhappy situation *now* **(B-)**, and leads to a happy ending *in the future* **(E+)**. Let's look at our two examples:

After the Smith-Corona story, you might say:

B- We, too, are at risk of falling behind the times.

M We need to recognize that now, and formulate a plan to adapt.

E+ So we will retain our place in the new economy.

The new story begins badly with your company at risk, proceeds with proactive actions in the middle, and ends with a more secure future.

The story about failing to hit numbers also can lead to a positive new story:

B- Now our division is at risk of being closed down.

M Let's prioritize and put all our resources toward our best marketing idea.

E+ So we can hit our numbers before the annual review.

This new story begins with your company at risk, its action in the middle is to focus on your best idea, and it ends with hitting the numbers before the next review.

Positive-to-negative stories can also be used to communicate empathy, to help someone recognize that he or she is not the only person to have suffered a particular pain or loss.

B+ The same thing happened to me two years ago. I had a great job,

M and I left it because I thought the switch was going to be a step up.

E- But it turned out to be a major backstep, and I realized I was going the wrong direction on the corporate ladder.

As soon as you're done sharing empathy through a negative story, it is time to move your audience forward toward a positive outcome using the classic negative-to-positive story. You might say:

B- So there I was in a worse position than I had been in a year earlier.

M I had no choice but to face my mistake. I found a career coach and made a new plan.

E+ Eventually I found my current position that I love.

Do you see how the first story used a positive-to-negative structure to communicate an understanding of the listener's situation, before telling a negative-to-positive story to inspire action in that person?

Human beings want to experience progress. One of the ways we achieve this is through stories that go from negative to positive. Stories that go from positive to negative can capture our attention, but in order to leave us in a positive state they need to proceed with new actions that continue the climb toward a higher level.

Once More With Feelings

One of the best ways to take something beyond information and into experience, is to assign it an emotion. People relate to information so much more when someone feels it. Let's take a look at a story first without, and then with, feelings:

B- Sales were down.

M We tried an out-of-the-box idea.

E+ Sales went up.

That's a complete story, and it's effective. However, it lacks any expression of emotions. Now look at the same story once you add feelings to the beginning and end.

B- Sales were down and everyone was deflated with worry.

M We tried an out-of-the-box idea.

E+ Now sales are up, and people are motivated and feel more secure.

Can you feel how much more compelling the brief story became when I added the human element of feelings? Note that I added feelings only to the beginning and end because their primary function is to help capture the experience of the change. There may have been lots of feelings in the experience of the middle (stress, excitement, frustration, pride, etc.), but what's important is that the actions taken brought you from "deflated with worry" to "motivated and secure." That's a good emotional argument for trying an out-of-the-box idea.

Messages are substantially more effective when they speak from the heart, rather than limiting the entire message to intellect and information. Intellect allows you to define a change and emotions allow you to feel it. Feelings help you care about facts. It's been statistically demonstrated that most decision-making is emotionally driven, so put emotion into your beginning and your end to create an *experience* of worse-to-better.

A "Middle" is Not an End In Itself

When you think about it, most of what you have to share is probably in the middle:

- Your services are actions that take clients somewhere
- Presentations share useful information about what an audience should know or do
- The new policy you're introducing is an action plan needing buy-in

- In a job interview, you share what you've done, and what you can do in the future
- An employee review is a look at what has and hasn't been accomplished

One of the most common design mistakes in corporate messages is being "middle-heavy" or worse, being *all* middle. People dive right into the middle, pitching their services, demanding change, requesting funds, justifying actions or pursuing assistance, without placing context around them. The beginning and end provide the framework necessary for understanding, and without them you have no journey.

How many times has your meeting room been filled with people arguing about *what to do?* This is usually because each person has a different beginning and end in mind, and actions look different, depending on their context. Align everyone to the same beginning and end, and you'll find it easier to agree on the middle to get there.

> *Only when an action has context does it have meaning.*
> *Action should change a negative situation to a positive one.*

Story Structure Works in Any Order

Director Quentin Tarantino proved with "Pulp Fiction" that if you jumble up the sequence of a story, it still works. In fact, he demonstrated that disguising the beginning/middle/end structure can also make stories more interesting.

Similarly, spoken messages can also work in any order, as long as you include all of the four components. Successful communication is more about being *complete* than being linear.

Let's look at a message about a stressed-out team, and try it out in different sequences. Here it is in a traditional order:

Beginning/Middle/End:

B- The team is really stressed because it is nearing its deadline, and has too many distractions.

M We designed a plan that will create blocks of time for people to focus,..

E+ ...and that will increase productivity and reduce stress.

This works really well. Now let's look at the exact same story sequenced differently:

Beginning/End/Middle:

B- The team is really stressed because it's nearing its deadline, with too many distractions.

E+ They need increased productivity with reduced stress...

M ...so we designed a plan to create blocks of time for people to focus.

This still works.

End/Beginning/Middle:

E+ The team really needs both increased productivity and less stress.

B- Right now, everyone is really stressed because of too many distractions, and they're nearing their deadline.

M So, we designed a plan to create blocks of time for people to focus.

Again, it still works.

Middle/End/Beginning:

M   I have a plan that will create blocks of time for people to focus.

E+ The team needs increased productivity and reduced stress...

B- ...because right now, the team is really stressed because its nearing its deadline and has too many distractions.

Once again, it works.

It doesn't really matter in what order the information comes. We've tried every combination, and they make sense as long as they are complete. And they motivate as long as there's context associated with action that bridges the beginning and the end.

I often do follow the traditional order. It's fine and logical. The most common alternate I use is the Beginning/End/Middle order because it sets up the context before I ask anyone to do anything:

B- Right now, you're worried that you're not ready for your presentation.

E+ You need to be confident, and prepared with all the skills to knock their socks off.

M   Let's do three sessions together, one on connecting to audiences, one on message design and one on dynamic delivery.

Messages that define the context first and then offer the action bridge are very effective selling messages.

Whatever your message, you have a lot of latitude in how you order your story, but you have only one structure. Map out your change and define the action that would cause it. Now tell it in any order you like.

The Fourth Part of Story: Who Is it About?

Who is the main character? Who is experiencing the change? Who is in the not-so-happy beginning situation and who is in the happy ending situation?

Main character is huge. Choosing the focus of the story, the main character, determines whether or not your audience will want to listen.

In designing messages for companies and business professionals, we discovered a common conflict. The presenters feel a need to talk about themselves to describe their business offering, so they make *themselves* the main character instead of focusing on the prospect they're trying to help.

Pete consistently designs every message around this question: "Who does my audience care about?" The answer to this question should be the main character.

Many of our corporate clients bring us in to help them prepare for some big-dollar, new-business pitch. Usually we discover that their presentation is designed around themselves instead of their clients. They start with the year their company was founded, and go on to bore their audience with unequivocal evidence to prove how great they are.

Quality and experience have their place, but a vendor isn't a main character the prospect is going to care about that much. The prospect cares about their own organization and the clients they serve. One of our biggest challenges is trying to switch the main character so that our client's sales pitch will matter to the prospect.

The process is straightforward enough. You simply think about who your audience cares about. Executives at a healthcare organization will certainly care about themselves, and also the doctors and nurses who work there. They most surely also care about their patients, as well as patient families, their board of directors and their financial contributors.

Any of these are candidates for a solid main character, based on that particular audience.

When we at SagePresence sell our services, we already know the Middle that we can provide, which is some version of presenting and communication training. So the middle of our message is very consistent. The change we describe is frequently about going from stage fright to stage presence, so the beginning and end stay the same. We make a point of picking main characters that our audience will care about. If we're talking to a room full of entrepreneurs, then our main character is business owners. If we're talking to career-minded professionals, *they* become our main character. If we're talking to dislocated workers, we refer to our main character as dislocated workers.

If you get the main character right, your audience will want to listen.

Selling Yourself

Sometimes the thing you're selling is yourself and the prospect is someone who needs you. When I worked in advertising, I was often selling myself as a creative person so that the client would ask for me specifically on their next project. Lawyers within a practice have to sell themselves to bring in business. Team members have to sell themselves to get promoted. And of course, there is the job interview.

I coached an executive who'd been out of work for a long time, and he was nervous while preparing for an executive job interview. He really clicked with the idea that the main character in a job interview was not himself, but the company interviewing him. He went to his interview with the idea that he was helping them with their problem of a C-level hole in their team. His interview was all about what the company needed and what kind of person was needed to address what they were facing and help them get where they wanted to go. At the end of the interview he said in a daring move, "What you're doing is so important that if you don't think

I'm the person for the job, I want to help you find the right fit. I know a lot of exceptional executive-level people, and if I'm not your person, I can connect you with one who might be."

With that statement, he became the right fit. He communicated that he cared passionately about them, the challenges they faced and the solutions they were looking for. And by putting that in front of his own needs, he showed the kind of selfless commitment they were seeking. It all came down to having the right main character and seeing the journey ahead.

Here are a few guidelines to ensure that you correctly choose your main character:

1. The Main Character Experiences the Change

Who is suffering in the not-so-happy beginning situation? Who feels happier in the end? This is the main character in your story.

2. The Main Character Is a Person or Group

Main characters are human beings with feelings and personalities. They can be individuals or groups of people. "Safety" is not a main character. The staff, who can experience danger and safety, is a more effective choice. The supply chain is not a main character either, but the "Supply Chain Division" could be, as could any group or individual who is affected by the supply chain process.

Why is this so critical? Because your audience is human, with human feelings. The story you tell needs to engage their feelings, and it can only do that if your main character can experience feelings.

An environmental organization we worked with was restoring the health of a lake located within a bird sanctuary. They wanted to make *the lake* the main character of a fundraising speech, but we steered them to make *the community* the main character. The quality of the lake was suffering, but the lake couldn't feel the environmental injury or experience any positive change. The community was a more correct main character. Why? Because the people who lived there and ran businesses near the lake were not benefiting from the potential that the lake could provide, including higher property values resulting from the restoration and more foot traffic near the stores. So we made the community the main character, and the environmental company successfully raised the money to restore the lake using that story.

If you are speaking about two entities who are working together, the main character becomes their *partnership*, or the group of people composed by multiple entities. You have room for creativity in how you package individuals and groups, but story works best when the main character is composed of a singular person, or a singular group of people who can have emotions.

3. Audience Must Care About the Main Character

Too many sales stories are mistakenly about the self-focused presenters who state: "We are so great. Therefore you should buy from us."

We can rely on prospects caring about *themselves* and the people *they* help. It's always more effective to find the other-centric angle and position your offering as the action to help them: "You are in a tough spot now, but with our help, you can be in a great situation."

To get an audience to listen to your message, make the main character someone they care about. Describe their change going from a difficult situation now to a better one in the *future*. Position you and your offering as the action in the middle that will take them there.

4. You Can Have Only One Main Character

The main character who starts your story *has* to be the main character who ends it. If you begin with a group of dislocated workers who hate networking, the story cannot end with a pitch about your great networking training. It can't start being about *them*, and end being about *you*. You can tell a story about a group who hated networking, and came to love it. And you can be in that story, as long as you stay away from the Beginning and End, where the main character is.

> **B-** Right now, based on the feedback from our survey, this is a room full of people who really hate networking.
>
> **M** Today's training, which has given hundreds of dislocated workers a reliable system to build relationships, will transform your approach to the job search.
>
> **E+** So you can have a fresh, positive experience as you network your way to new possibilities.

In this story, the group of dislocated workers is the main character, appearing in the Beginning and End. You only showed up in the Middle of the story, offering services.

You Are the Hero in the Middle

In your presentation, you are in the middle of the story, guiding the main character to move away from a less-than-ideal situation. That makes you the *hero* of the story, the one who helps the prospect face their issues and get where they want to be.

You are helping them with actions that take them where they want to go. Your presentation is other-centric—it's about them.

In selling, the conundrum is that you are essentially *asked* by your prospects to pitch your own value, after which you may get some money. "Tell us about yourself," they will say. This can trick you into thinking you are the focus.

Thinking about yourself heroically may sound a bit over-inflated when you don't want to be stuck on yourself. But 'hero positioning' tends to boost your self-perception, and positions you nobly within a story that's really about *them*.

Pete and I think of ourselves as supporting heroes for the people like you who we serve. When people ask what SagePresence does, we say:

B- Business professionals find us because they have some sort of stage fright in the way of having authentic confidence under pressure.

M We bring movie skills to help them connect to audiences, develop great messages and deliver them dynamically.

E+ In the end, they have 'stage presence' and excitement to take on what scares them.

This is a contagious concept. When we position ourselves as supporting heroes that are helping the audience we're speaking to, the audience changes. They begin to view themselves as the helping heroes for the people to whom *they* offer services. It's a healthy role to foster— and an improved way to sell.

> *Be a hero and support your main characters*
> *with everything you've got.*

Structure Is for Both Heart and Mind

Describing a change in *situation* provides context, making information meaningful. Describing a change in *emotion* creates an experience, inspiring motivation and drive.

Decision-making is about both logic and emotion. In fact, studies indicate that decisions are made far more by emotion than logic. Your story structure model needs to address both head and heart, providing a rational argument through the situational change, and an emotional argument through the change of feelings. Together, *situation* and *feeling* are more human and more powerful than either would be alone.

> *Situation and feeling combined deliver a message*
> *your audience will understand and experience.*

Finding the Story in the Moment

Recently I worked with someone in the engineering industry preparing for a sales pitch. Under presentation pressure, his attention was circling inward, back on himself, and he was becoming extremely self-aware. Although he's a very smart man who has spoken for decades, his automatic process of talking was becoming quite difficult and he was self-consciously paying attention to every word and speaking as though each one was its own sentence.

His boss tried to help by giving him some language to learn and recite. The very sight of this nervous man reading the eloquent words of a senior marketing exec was a bizarre juxtaposition. This man knew his subject, but he clearly had no connection to the words he was forcing out of his mouth. Fortunately, this was just a rehearsal and we still had time to help.

Think about this:

- How many times a day do you design, memorize and recite something? Not every day, right?
- How many times a week do you design, memorize and recite something? Not every week, correct?
- How many times a year do you plan, script, memorize and recite something important? Maybe a few.

At most, the average professional formally speaks only a handful of times each year. And those are the big moments, often the really important ones.

Now consider this:

- How many times a year do you *answer a question*? Would you need a super-computer to process this answer?
- How many times a month do you answer a question? Still impossible to calculate.
- How many times a week? Or a day? Still a big number, right?
- •Okay, here's the real question I'm building to: *How many times in an hour do you typically answer a question?* I'll bet it's quite a few.

So clearly, you're more practiced at answering questions than you are writing, memorizing and reciting speeches. Whenever Pete and I are looking to help one of our coaching clients achieve normal dialogue, all

we have to do is ask them a question and even the nervous person seems to snap out of his or her shell to talk to us normally.

If speaking extemporaneously—the way you do when you answer a question on a typical day—is one of your most practiced skills, and since designing, memorizing and reciting scripted dialogue is your least practiced skill—why are you bringing your *least-practiced skill* to your *most-important moments?*

Instead, why don't you create a list of questions related to your subject and answer them for your audience? Try this:

1. Start by creating notes about what you want to say.
2. Turn those notes into questions.
3. Read the questions in your mind as if someone in the audience had asked them.
4. Answer them out loud to the audience.

Here are some examples of questions you could use to cue yourself. I bet you could talk for several minutes or more to each one of these questions, without so much as a single rehearsal.

- What issue brings us together today?
- Who is in what challenging situation right now?
- What needs to happen for them?
- What better place could that take them to?

We tried this with the nervous engineer after he had finished reading the senior marketing exec's words. What we'd just seen was him looking at his paper as he read the other guy's words, looking up only once for a nervous glance to an audience he didn't really see anyway. His test audience was fidgeting with worry, fearing a colossal failure and the loss of a big project.

Pete and I did not want to spook this already nervous presenter. So first we praised the engineer for bravely working his way to the end of the prepared speech and then we asked him three questions:

- What is the challenging situation right now for the client?
- What needs to be done?
- And what will the better situation be for the client after these things get done?

With no more prompting, the man forgot that he was presenting, looked out to the group and answered the questions. He didn't state the questions, he only gave the answers, and instantly his dialogue became normal. It wasn't flawless, but in a way it was *perfect,* because he was showing the audience who he really was. The words came from him, and sounded natural. Through his 'average' words, his expertise flowed.

Developing natural dialogue is easily accomplished by abandoning the memorization process and simply providing answers to questions you ask yourself. It's attained by designing a sequence of questions that follows story structure, as the questions above do. Each question inspires a little bubble of content. Talk in one bubble until you feel you've covered that part. Then silently ask yourself the next question and talk in that bubble for a while. Our example had a beginning bubble, a middle bubble, and an end bubble and his presentation was made as though he were in a Q&A-styled interview.

'Q&A-style notes' make you instantly capable
of achieving natural dialogue.
You can be 'normal you' in front of a group,
while communicating logically.

An interesting side-benefit of this Q&A notes strategy, as compared to using traditional bullet-point notes, is that there's virtually no difference between your approach to a speech and to the Q&A after the speech.

It takes the 'gear shifting' out of the equation. Presentation and Q&A will suddenly feel about the same, except that you are the one asking the questions during your speech, and the audience will be asking them during your Q&A. One becomes the practice for the other, and your readiness to respond to audience questions will be primed during your presentation.

Q&A-style notes balance improvisation and structure
to bring you the benefits of both.

Summary: Message Design

Story is not a sequence of words, but a structural system that allows you to make sense of any information by giving it context that your audience will care about.

All stories are about exactly one main character—individual or group—who undergoes a change from negative to positive. The story always travels from negative to positive, except for an occasional cautionary tale. If you tell a cautionary tale, it is your obligation to follow it up with a negative-to-positive story to motivate a change for the better.

Story structure is wired into human cognition. It's reliable, efficient and will lead to a kind of clarity and power that will, more than any beautifully crafted words, influence the moment. You wanted the magic words, but we've given you something even better. We've given you a message structure that makes your ordinary words magic.

One more set of bars is now removed from the your cage of safety. Not knowing what to say had led you to hide from expressing yourself authentically. Before, you had to open your mouth to discover where your words would take you, so holding back gave you one thing you could be certain about.

Now you have one simple equation as your map and compass to navigate the process of speaking from your heart. Your new security is the reliable structure of story. With story, you have wings, and you can carry that security with you, as you fly into a world of possibilities. It really is this simple.

Someone your audience cares about is in a problematic situation.
Something needs to happen to take them to a better place.

Chapter 6

Dynamic Delivery

SCARLETT: Sir, you should have
made your presence known.

Script from the movie
"Gone With the Wind"

How can you be more interesting when you present? How do you stop yourself from freezing up, shutting down or flattening out?

How can you free your personality from its instinct to hide?

Sometimes you can tell your personality is locked away and you can't find the key. If you want to be able to engage and maintain your audience, you're going to have to find it, so you can be dynamic enough to capture their attention. Dynamism is a product of body language, which is a catch-all for voice tone, gesture, posture, facial expressions, the way you move, your proximity to audience and nearly anything related to how your personality shines through—all the how-you-say-it stuff.

Dynamism makes a statement in itself. It's body language for, "I'm more than the sum of my words." Sadly, the lack of dynamism communicates that there's less here than meets the ears. So, even if your message represents the information that your audience desperately needs, you are doing your audience a disservice by failing to deliver that information with dynamism—because they won't be interested in hearing it.

Dynamism is definable and attainable, and every personality type has access to charisma, although clearly not everyone knows how to find either of them. As much as we think of these two qualities as elusive, you need little more than your own natural personality to achieve them.

Charisma results from a mix of several qualities covered in this book. You connect deeply with people regardless of the circumstances, allowing chemistry to build while remaining other-centered. On top of that, you add dynamism.

What you're dealing with is not something missing as much as it is something that hides when you're under pressure. Dynamic speakers have found a way to shoo their personality out of the cage even under the pressure of performance. This seemingly rare breed of communicator is brave enough to be expressive where the rest of us shut down or hold back.

Dynamism is being *yourself*, like you are when you forget about *you*.

Most of the time, you're focused on something else, with occasional moments in front of a mirror. Unfortunately, audiences reflect their speaker like a mirror, making it hard to act like you're in autopilot mode in front of them when you're not. Performance pressure makes you self-aware, which is the opposite of autopilot. It puts too much attention on you to act normal.

To be dynamic, you need to be able to forget about yourself, tap into your emotions and feel what you say. With emotion, every word can have a magical quality. Without emotion, every word will at best be unadorned information. If you let yourself go numb in response to pressure, you'll have less ability to be expressive at a time when you need more personality.

Dynamism involves your body. It doesn't come from words, it comes from you as you speak them. It is something for you *to be*, more than it is something *to do*. When you're dynamic, people fully give their attention, and when you're not, they split their attention between you and other thoughts, like a teenager daydreaming of his own story in an English literature class.

The Language of Dynamism

Think of yourself as bilingual. The language of words delivers your thoughts. The language of the body expresses your feelings.

When you present, your body language can tell your audience that you are "quite certain," or "really struggling," or "quite passionate about this particular point."

Body language from your audience informs you as well. "You just lost me," or "I'm not buying that," or "I agree completely!" Often their body language will tell you more than their words do. The exhilarated "a-ha" face an audience member makes when having a eureka moment can communicate more than the words, "I'm having a breakthrough."

Words speak only when you talk. Body language speaks all the time. Words deliver a finite amount of data, but body language speaks *volumes*. You're usually not consciously aware that this language is being sent and received, even though it's always going out and usually getting in. You're broadcasting information about yourself, and perceiving it in others around you. It affects all people.

Great speakers embrace this and let the language of their body do most of the work. They let it flow more freely than novice speakers, making it obvious to their audience that they are seasoned under pressure.

Dynamic speakers are whole-body communicators. Does this sound out of reach, like something you could never be? I don't think so. You already are a whole-body communicator in moments that don't matter. But when the feeling of vulnerability hits you, your expression seizes up, like when a squirrel spots a hawk.

You feel vulnerable when your emotions are showing so you hold still in an unconscious attempt to try to shut down your body language and stop it from revealing your anxiety. But that's impossible. It just doesn't work. You fail to turn off that which has no off-switch, and your fear shows anyway through the bars of your cage.

Neutralizing your emotions purifies the fear by stripping out the passion. I prefer a mix of fear and passion over just the fear, but a lot of people are willing to snuff out their passion if only to reduce their fear a little.

Please don't suffocate your own personality. It will leave you with only stilted dialogue, which will come out flat and perhaps a little fast. Leave the anxiety the way it is and add passion to it.

This chapter will show you three easy paths to doing this:

1. Finding your natural personality (*a thinking solution*).
2. Tapping your emotions (*a feeling solution*).
3. Freeing your body to express (*a physical solution*).

Being dynamic is all about finding the natural you.
Feel your words and set your body free to express them.

Dynamism from the Director's Chair

A film director relies on several elements to ensure a good performance in a movie: a well-written script, effective direction to help the performer interpret that script and an expressive delivery to trigger feelings in the audience.

Since a film's tight production timeline can't afford chaos, a rigid chain of command regulates the sequence of information flow. The writer can't direct the actors, but he can influence the director. The director instructs the actors, who can bargain with the director. Sometimes, influence from the actor leads the director to talk to the writer who will then change the lines on the set. But if the writer starts directing the actors, or the actors start changing lines on their own, chaos results. Everything in film has to flow through the director.

In presenting, *mind* is the writer and *heart* is the director, so *body* is the actor. No matter how smart you are, everything flows from the heart. No matter how limber you are, you will not express yourself freely or authentically unless your body is directed to do so by the heart. The information flow is just as rigid in your body as it is on a film set.

But sometimes pressure knocks your heart senseless, so your emotions go numb, leaving your mind and body directionless. This can be tragic in your attempt to be dynamic, because your mind happens to be a terrible stand-in director for body language. If you doubt that, think back to the last time you bumped into someone you didn't like at a social function. You mocked up a friendly show, but people could tell you didn't like each other.

On a film set, if the director loses his marbles, another director is put in place but obviously there's no equivalent in your body when the pressure strikes and your feelings are suddenly AWOL. Fortunately, there is a remedy, and it requires rehearsing with mind, heart and body together.

Many people just think through what they're going to say, possibly visualizing their performance as if it were the same as rehearsing. But that's not enough because you want your body to know what to do in the worst case, which is fear-induced emotional absence.

When connected as a chain, information flows from mind to heart then through body in a very rigid sequence. Rehearsing all three together allows any one of them to be an understudy of the other two. Rehearse completely, so if head, heart or body lets you down under pressure, the other two can cover the base.

The challenges that shut dynamism down and the solutions that bring it back are more or less the same for public speaking, on-camera presenting, talking in a meeting and having a high-stakes conversation. At the end of this chapter, we'll explore some differences between these four venues. Until then, I'm going to connect the dots mostly to the challenge of public speaking. This is the environment in which most people recognize their need for dynamism. Learning in that realm teaches principles for all of them. Master expressing on the stage and you'll be able to do it on camera, in meetings and in conversation.

The dynamism you want is already in you as it needs to be, but a few things in your wiring can trip you up. Let's look at three dynamic villains, and then work to overcome them.

#1: Observation Interferes with Normal Functioning

When your doctor asks you to breathe normally, you don't know how. How were you breathing before? Like any behavior, your breathing changed when you paid attention to it. Body language is like that.

So how can you try to be yourself when "trying" is essentially the obstacle itself? It's hard because it's paradoxical. The movie "Hugo" has a scene where two children, Hugo and Isabelle, are trying to evade the watchful eyes of their opponent, a constable at a train station. Hugo says to Isabelle, "Act normal," but both children begin walking awkwardly with a lumbering gait that instantly draws the constable's attention. Self-awareness is the cause of their wooden performance.

Anything observed is changed by the observation. Scientists say that even on the atomic level, observing subatomic particles with an electron microscope somehow changes their behavior. While my unscientific brain cannot quite grasp how viewing an atom would change anything,

I am keenly aware of how my self-observation changes me. When I get thrown into neutral by self-awareness, I try to "play act" myself, to talk like I talk, walk the way I walk and think the way I think. Like trying to breathe normally for the doctor, I don't know how to do it.

#2: Turning Off Fear Equals Turning Off Passion

When you allow yourself to *feel* under pressure, you *will* feel vulnerable and vulnerability can be the trigger to your "freeze" instincts, like what squirrels have when a predator hawk circles overhead. These instincts give you only one message: "Don't move a muscle. Don't show 'em nuthin'. If they see you move, you are in danger."

Audiences won't be influenced unless they feel your passion, but your instincts are telling you to hide it. You have to increase your tolerance of the vulnerable feeling that comes with the attention of other people and the self-consciousness that this attention can inspire. People put a lot of needless energy toward numbing themselves, shutting the whole system down to protect themselves. The remedy:

- Practice moments of self-awareness—checking in during "auto-pilot" moments—so you can be self-aware without spooking yourself.
- Practice triggering emotions to get used to the activity of feeling on demand.

This will help you learn to tolerate more self-awareness with less self-consciousness.

#3: When You Need to Show More, Instincts Say, Show Less

We are used to reading and interpreting body language up close and personal, from someone right in front of us. This is harder to see from the back row of a presentation, so while stress and pressure are leading you to want to show less, this is precisely the time you need to show more. Expressing more visibly can amp you up to show higher passion and commitment in any setting.

More expression is required to inspire people who are farther away.

At the same time, authenticity is critical. Audiences want genuine feelings, and want them shown as freely and visibly as they are in conversation. Activating genuine emotion is what screen actors specialize in because the camera is right up in their face. As a speaker you need the authenticity of the close up—only bigger—for the wide shot that those in the back row will see.

The rehearsal practice of pushing bigger, freer expressions helps you achieve a level that will basically look *normal* to the audience that is farther away. In this practice, you'll be building muscle memory for your expressive performance, and you'll rehearse without a camera, mirror, or audience—free from judgment. This is how you'll create a natural and intimate conversation experience with your audience.

This idea runs counter to instinct, because the perceived risks of public speaking make it feel unsafe, and therefore less intimate. When you feel unsafe, your protective instincts kick in, and you don a fear-induced poker-face.

We've all seen speakers flatten out once on stage. When this happens, any nervous twitches and 'tells' seem doubly visible. A flinch won't show much when it's diluted by passion. But when your expression is as still as a lake on a windless morning, those awkward twitches become ripples visible from shore to shore.

This is why you need to practice generating true feelings with more expressiveness. As for me, the more I commit to a higher level of genuine feelings and expressions in rehearsal, the more effective I am at accessing them in the real event. This is how I present myself so confidently—my nervous twitches and 'tells' very well may be there, but proportionate to my passion, they are well obscured.

My expressive system has been strengthened by this practice, as though additional circuit breakers have been added to my heart to handle more emotional voltage. And the practice has done for my body what stretching does for a dancer. Physically, I've gotten used to looser, more fluid, bigger expressions that are appropriate for the world outside, where before I restricted my expressions to a range suitable for a very small cage.

Dynamic Foes in Review

I've described three scenarios that impact dynamism:

1. Self-observation interferes with expression.
2. Suppression of fear stifles passion.
3. When you need more expression, it's harder to access.

Because nearly everyone contends with these three challenges in a presentation, improvement in any one of these zones will be a win for you. It will put you heads above the crowd, even if you only improve slightly. Forget mastery. Improvement is enough. Ongoing improvement is ideal, because you are perpetually increasing your chances to win.

A Definition of Dynamism

What exactly is dynamism?

A lot of people think dynamism is high energy. This exuberance can often grab your initial attention, but after a moment or two, if the speaker stays at this level, its value will diminish to little more than white noise.

It's easy to confuse high energy with dynamism, even though low-energy presenters might also be engaging. Very early in my career I watched an elderly woman speak at a conference, and she had low energy but high dynamism. She was feeble and needed help to the podium, which she then clutched for balance. She barely had enough lungpower to speak into the microphone, yet she held each and every person in the house captive. Something about her drew us in, and didn't let go. Was it her voice tone? Her emotion? Her timing? I marveled at her commanding presence, but her source of power was unclear. Dynamism *must* be something other than energy, I concluded. My work in the coming years showed me the principle she was exploiting, and how simple it was, next to the complexity and depth of her impact.

Dynamism is: Change.

What seems to define dynamic delivery is *change*. If you change stuff, you're dynamic. When it comes to delivery, change is anything in one moment that is different from what it was in another moment. If you don't change anything, you're flat, or white noise—static.

White noise can be quiet, like the kind of noise that helps you sleep. Or it can be loud, like the hum of an air conditioner that eventually you don't hear anymore. People who live in heavy traffic areas don't hear it after a while, because anything consistent can eventually be ignored. A TV is harder to ignore because it keeps changing: Bright shot, dark shot, loud scene, quiet scene, stationary shot, moving shot, running, talking, commercial break. Audiences tune out whatever drones on. Variety shakes them awake and elevates their attention. Each time something changes you perk up and get drawn in. That is why those annoying after-market car alarms are so hard to ignore. First they call out a classic alarm sound, then it's a "whoop-whoop," a "bee-boop-bee-boop," then "chirp-chirp-chirp," and finally they make a long sliding whistle sound from low to high pitch. There's no way to ignore them, because the sounds keep changing.

Change is what made the elderly woman powerful. She did not have much energy, but she changed things as she talked, from certain words she would unexpectedly drag out, to the occasional pause she would hold onto for a seeming eternity, to the way she would switch from informational to dramatic in tone, with different feelings showing on her face.

When I hear a presenter, I want more than a flatline voice and two-dimensional delivery. Give me 3-D and tears! Give me laughter! Give me change!

Take responsibility for your own passion. Breathe some life into your subject. Passion is everywhere. Wait...*everywhere*, but in your presentation. Listeners expect you to find the passion in your subject. If you can't find it, they won't find it either. A passionate speaker can relight the latent passion in an audience, like relighting a candle.

Light up your audience. No speaker wants an audience member to zone out, stealing their presentation time for daydreaming, writing to-do lists or processing something else like a text message. Speakers want all eyes on them, and every thought focusing on the subject of their speech.

Pursue 100 percent attention from your audience. Dynamism establishes attention and refreshes it by creating constant change.

Pete and I gave a series of three back-to-back presentations to a company needing to boost sales through new prospects and existing clients. The first session covered networking for new prospects. The second focused on customer service communication to position new work. The final part of the series revealed how to win competitive sales presentations. Each event was four hours long, spanning a day and a half. Some people were in all three sessions, and others were in one or two, so we had to repeat our introductions along with some content that applied to all three presentations. I was worried about holding anyone's attention for that much time, especially given the overlap. For all these reasons, Pete and I were particularly committed to being dynamic. We changed certain aspects of our performance, such as:

- Words we chose to use and the way we said them
- Places where we were energetic or calm
- Our emotional display
- When we chose to use the board or a Powerpoint
- Which one of us was talking
- Where in the room we stood
- When we were interactive or presentational

Even through our third presentation, our audience showed us engaged, excited faces. After the close, as I allowed myself a quiet sigh of relief, one participant came up to us and said, "I'm a very impatient person. The company recently made me go to a speech, and in that case, I struggled to stick it out for ninety minutes. *But with you guys, I was on the edge of my seat for twelve hours*, and I would listen to more."

Our content was good and we worked to make it relevant, but without refreshing it with constant change we would never have been able to hold their attention that long.

Dynamism: The Activity

The impact of dynamism is amazing. But there's nothing amazing about dynamism. It's simple, and I'd like to make the concept visual for you.

This is a flat line. It is not dynamic. This is the line you wouldn't want on the hospital EEG measuring your vitals—and you wouldn't want your audience to see you as one either. If you don't change anything about your performance as a speaker, you're a flat line.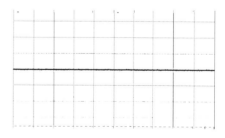

This is a dynamic line. It rises up and drops down, and then up and down again, resembling a dragon's back. Notice how much more dynamic it is than the first line.

You can make that line even more dynamic by giving it higher highs and lower lows, or by making the highs and lows unpredictable.

Dynamism = Change.

If you change 'stuff,' you're dynamic and if you don't, you're not. If you change things unpredictably, you're even more dynamic. Highs and lows with unpredictable randomness is all you need to keep your audience's attention.

The only step remaining is to figure out what to change. Here's a list of the things you can change. Read and remember, then practice changing them. This will increase your dynamism.

The "Things-to-Change" List

There are only six dynamics that we consider at SagePresence. Each one represents a zone for expressive potential. And each zone has a potential barrier. For each item, you want to randomly practice higher highs and lower lows. This increases dynamism. When you change *any one item* on the list, other items on the list also change.

These are the six dynamics:

1. **Eye contact.** Who you look at, and for how long.
2. **Volume.** How loud and soft you are.
3. **Tempo.** How fast and slow you talk.

4. **Gesture.** Talking with your hands, and when they are at rest.

5. **Movement.** How, when and where you walk and stop.

6. **Emotion.** The different feelings you experience.

Only Six Dynamics?

People ask us questions:

"Why such a short list? We can think of many aspects of human expression. What about pitch and tone?"

"How about facial expression? Why isn't that on the list?"

"Wait a second. I can smile if I want, and I don't need to change my emotions for that, do I?"

We respond:

Well, what determines pitch or tone? Emotion does, don't you think? It's number six on the list.

What determines your facial expressions? Emotion does, and once again it's number six on our list. Sure you can smile, but you can't look happy without being happy. Have you looked at your grade-school photos? When you manually try to do expressions, they often express something other than what you intend. Something artificial happens when you try to imitate what comes naturally. On the flip side, if you're happy, it's hard to hide because your face responds authentically to the feeling. Remember trying to look serious in high school when you were about to burst out laughing? That's why your teacher singled you out, and asked you if you had something to share with the rest of the class.

Photogenic people tap their emotions, letting feelings create their expressions authentically. For those less photogenic, a thing called camera-phobia will temporarily numb their emotions—forcing them to operate their face like a puppet's—and it shows. This is important to both screen actors and business presenters; emotion is the only reliable control for authentic facial expression.

Dynamic number six takes care of almost everything. That's why our list is so short.

Heart and Body—Practicing the Dynamic Duo

Heart is to body what Batman is to Robin. Batman is the hero, and Robin is the sidekick. They must practice together so that Robin can anticipate and assist with all of Batman's super moves, and every once in a while, Batman gets in a bind, so Robin is there as the backup hero. That's the dynamic duo.

Similarly, heart and body are an expressive dynamic duo. The heart's emotional power is clearly the superhero, and body is the sidekick. They have to practice expression together in order for the body to anticipate the heart's power moves. When you open yourself up to feel your words, often the power comes, but sometimes it doesn't.

Heart may be a superhero, but it is also as temperamental as a rock star, and sometimes refuses to come out of its trailer for the big show. When that happens, you're out there on your own, holding a bag of words with no sense of the beat or timing. Numb is not a good feeling in front of a crowd, as much as we think we'd prefer it to fear. When emotions go blank, ideas are expressed without passion, and they fall flat.

Like Batman and Robin, heart and body will have practiced together. So if heart doesn't join body on stage, and your head knows the show must go on, then body has to step up and save the day. It's not ideal, but it doesn't have to be a showstopper either—not if body has learned heart's rock star moves. Body, meet heart. Heart, meet body. Rehearse together, and the two of you will be okay no matter what. That way, your head can be free to focus on your words.

Building Muscle Memory of Dynamism

Athletes talk about muscle memory. It's when they've practiced something enough that their bodies know what to do without paying attention, allowing them to think strategically instead of tactically. Dancers speak of muscle memory too. Presenters who practice speaking, feeling and expressing through their bodies build a similar muscle memory, so that body can practically operate itself.

A friend of mine gave a beautiful eulogy at his father's funeral. He was proud of himself, and for good reason, but later commented that while he'd practiced many times, his practice consisted only of reading his speech silently from an easy chair. It felt so different when he stood up and actually used his voice, and that led to a few awkward starts and stops. He vowed the next time he faced a speech to practice his actual delivery out loud, as a true rehearsal.

Emotion and heart will take care of everything dynamic from the inside out. But you also want to clear the way for feelings to show, and you can do that by mechanically practicing body language with some key drills. You might think of it like the Tin Man with his oiling can, or a runner stretching before a sprint, or a soccer player practicing kicks and throws until the muscles remember how they should move without specific instruction. The isolated practice of eye contact, volume, tempo, movement and gesture, will help loosen your body and teach you expressive patterns that encourage your heart to shine through.

Our drill strategy begins with the first five dynamic drills and works up to emotion. The drillls pre-wire your body so your feelings more easily show, and if you hit an emotional wall on stage, you'll have the muscle memory to run your body until your heart kicks back in and feels again.

I gave a keynote to a group of parents of kids with disabilities. My job was to inspire them with my own experience as a worried parent with a child facing some serious health challenges. This was the most powerful material I could ever talk about and it brought me to tears every time in rehearsal. I had done it all right: Practicing in advance, memorizing the flow of the main points and avoiding rehearsal on the actual day to save my performance for the stage. I was excited about it, fully expecting my emotions to supercharge every word. But on the long drive to the lodge where the event was being held, I got lost and my GPS wasn't getting a signal. The fear of being late knocked me off my game.

I was relieved when I showed up with ample time, but I still felt the stress. I didn't take the time to rustle up the proper appreciation in the hustle it took to find the right room. So when I took the stage...I felt nothing. I was totally taken off-guard. I had not even considered that I might blow an emotional circuit breaker when I was sharing something so personal. My stories were sad enough to topple the sturdiest of oaks, yet I was not the least bit stirred by any of them. This terrified me.

Forced to rely on the mechanics of dynamism to make the audience feel what I *should* have been feeling, I relied on a muscle memory that I'd built during rehearsal. Because of being emotional in rehearsals, my body knew what to do. I felt myself moving in the right ways, similarly to when I had genuinely felt it, and that gradually triggered a return of my emotions. Like Robin rescuing Batman, my body jump-started my emotions, at least at a few key points.

At the end of that presentation, I was very worried that I might have let the audience down. I thought about quickly running off stage and to the car to avoid "death by faint praise." But before I could target the nearest exit, I couldn't believe it—I was surprised by a standing ovation and a line of people forming to thank me. That day's success can be attributed to the practice described below, integrating mind, heart and body.

Dynamic Instruction

We're going to start working the six dynamics that invoke heart, body and mind. First, we're going to get your body out of the cage, then your heart. Think of the first five as soccer drills for expressiveness and the sixth—emotion—as the ultimate supercharger for dynamism.

It's normal for one of these practices to click with you more than another, making a particularly profound impact. Everyone is unique, and each activity stretches you differently than it will stretch someone else. Together, all six will elevate you way beyond your current level of dynamism.

Note that these are just drills. Don't worry about them in your presentation, or you'll pull your attention off your audience and put it back on yourself—opposite of our goal. So practice these as drills in rehearsal, and forget about them during your make-or-break moments.

Dynamic Drill #1: Eye Contact

Dynamism is as simple as delivering one single sentence
to one single person
before switching randomly to another person.

Never speak to a crowd again, no matter how many people are in front of you. Instead, form a one-to-one relationship as you share a single sentence with someone specific. Create an *undivided* experience for the duration of that sentence.

Speak to only one person at a time. But over the course of your presentation, make a point to get to everyone. Cover them in zones, switching as randomly as possible—up front, way back, on either side and in the middle. Try to interact with each individual in the audience for at least one sentence. Even if the group is too big for you to literally achieve this, this method will create an experience of connection for everyone.

Eye contact is your big chance for connections.

Everyone knows that eye contact is powerful. True eye contact is not merely looking at people; it's actually *seeing* them. Appreciation is a great practice to help you see them and emotionally *reach* them so you can have chemistry with them.

One of my college professors made direct, appreciative eye contact with me in the midst of a huge room full of students. We clearly had a unique chemistry, so I concluded that he cared about me far beyond any of the other ninety students, who probably felt the exact same way, because they would have had their own unique chemistry with him *during their sentence* with him. My connection with this professor was genuine and personal, but it wasn't *exclusive*. He genuinely appreciated all his students.

At the dinner table, happy hour or in a meeting, practice appreciating people as you practice direct eye contact one sentence at a time.

There are two key benefits to dynamic eye contact.

A single sentence is enough time to forge an appreciative connection, and doing so will build dynamism in two ways.:

1. Every sentence is a different length, so if you follow the one-sentence-per-person approach, eye contact will not become a repetitive pattern. It will *change* because each sentence is a different length.
2. Each person you look at will be in a different area of the room, which means that every sentence will provide the audience with a different view of your face.

Through our coaching, we are proud to have transformed seemingly timid speakers into visually confident speakers without actually changing anything else but eye contact. Was the person truly timid? Did we really lead them to confidence? How would I know? The *perceived confidence* effect comes from reaching out to people with eye contact. And in this case, audience perception is all that matters.

A wonderful side-effect of the one-sentence-per-person technique is that people with little to no sense of timing often gain a sudden boost in their pacing because we're encouraging them to take a moment to find and connect with the next person between sentences.

A clever client with a wonderfully dry sense of humor had developed some smart content peppered with subtle jokes. He was pleasant to listen to but his flow was monotonous, leaving him unable to hit any of the beats that would have made his clever remarks funny. His content was a series of rhetorical questions, which he would ask, then answer.

Jokes, like dramatic stories, need to be set up before being paid off, and that requires a big pause between them. But he just tossed out the question—and answered it immediately, making it sound like information, leaving his wit unnoticed. Working with timing and flow had not been our target in eye contact drills. However, the silent gaps he left each time he finished one sentence then found the next person and started the next sentence put the proper timing into his setups and payoffs—and people began to laugh.

Scanning is for the birds.

For an audience, good eye contact should have a hand-delivered feeling. From the presenter's point of view, think of it like *feeding the birds*.

I was in London with my wife on a night I had a presentation. We noticed a street vendor selling bird food in small bags so we bought one. The melody of "Feed the Birds" from "Mary Poppins" was looping pleasantly in my mind. We threw the feed out on the lawn in front of us, and the birds fought over it. A few of the weaker birds were too slow to get any food.

When the bag was empty and the competition was over, Kim and I looked at each other, feeling disheartened. Our intent in feeding the birds was to create a warm experience for ourselves by giving the gift of food to the birds. But the scuffle wasn't particularly pleasant. It seemed to bring out the birds' meanness and we felt sad for the ones that got none. We bought a second bag and tried a new strategy: we varied where we threw the crumbs. The feathered crowd spread, unable to predict where the next crumb would land.

At that point, they started looking like an audience, and we targeted birds individually—hand delivering a single crumb to a single bird, making it pretty easy to ensure every bird received its fair share.

Through a bird's eye lens, I think that must have been a good audience experience. Kim and I felt warm inside and the birds were attentive and respectful. That night when I presented, I caught myself scanning the crowd, randomly flitting from person to person. I was feeling disconnected from the people, and it dawned on me to model eye contact on the pattern that Kim and I had used to feed the birds. Instantly, I felt the power of connection exponentially grow.

Try this, and your presentation will feed a content-hungry crowd with your thoughts:

1. Deliver one sentence to one person before randomly selecting another.
2. Imagine that each sentence is a valuable nugget of content and you're hand-delivering each crumb to someone.
3. Break the audience into zones (front, middle, back, left, center, right) and bounce unpredictably into each zone.
4. Switch in the pause between sentences, allowing the

silent pause, then starting the new sentence with the next person.

5. Try to pick different people until you've spent a sentence with every person in the room.

Extra Credit: **Make silent eye contact before starting.**

When you first step up to speak, see if you can resist saying anything.

Not one word. Immediately connect silently and *with appreciation* to four people for about three seconds per person, then speak to the fourth person.

This will feel very uncomfortable the first few times you try it, so you need to practice it—or you won't do it. Silent connections give you *ownership* of the moment. Try to *own the moment* every time you present. Watch me speak at ThinkBig Education in London on www.SagePresence.com/speaking. When you see me do this you'll sense the relationships I'm silently forming with individuals before I even say a word. This particular speaking sample was probably the most scared I'd ever been in a speech, but you won't notice my knees knocking. You'll see that through my silent connections of eye contact and appreciation before I spoke, *I had them at hello.*

Dynamic Drill #2: Volume

*Dynamism is as simple as being loud sometimes,
and soft at other times.*

Loud captures attention and shakes people awake. It emphasizes whatever you're saying. Soft draws people forward toward the edge of their seats, drawing their utmost attention. Volume is the dynamic that seems to impact the audience's perception of your energy.

Don't over-think it. Practice speaking as loud as you can and as soft as you can, alternating sentence by sentence, for several practice runs as you rehearse.

It sounds simple, because it is. And the benefit it creates is enormous. Change your volume sentence by sentence, or randomly, and your dynamism will increase in numerous ways beyond volume. Push both ends of the spectrum. Things improve the more times you switch. The louder the loud and the softer the soft, the more dynamic you'll be.

It doesn't seem to matter *when* you're loud or soft. It doesn't have to align with your content. It seems that the change itself makes you instantly more dynamic by creating a spectrum of highs and lows. This we predicted. Our surprise was that when you create a change spectrum with volume, the rest of your body language seems to join in on the fun, and a lot of other things change as well. People who change their volume tend to move more, show more emotions, gesture more and fire up their audiences more.

Practice loud and soft intentionally in rehearsals, and then forget about it in your actual presentation. Because you will have given your body the muscle memory of volume dynamism, you'll be loud when it feels right, and soft when it feels right.

Speakers who change volume often seem very energetic.
This keeps audiences energized as they listen.

Loud has emotional power.

One reason that volume is associated with high energy is that emotion is often used as the fuel to generate a high volume. We tell people in a workshop to get loud and without realizing it, they tend to increase their emotions to do it. Since emotion is the ultimate dynamic fuel, the participants instantly become more expressive, beyond what I would expect from a simple volume change. It completely engages audiences.

The secret power of soft.

When we tell people to say something quietly and they do, their words sound more important, *as though they are sharing a secret.* The content doesn't actually need to be secret-worthy. The boost in perceived significance comes from the whisper, and the audience can't resist leaning in and listening hard.

Getting started.

Try this: Make your first sentence *really loud.* People who resist volume change tend to never get much louder than their very first words. So if you open VERY LOUD, you'll have a better shot at maintaining a loud/soft dynamic range.

When I rehearse, I often belt out my first statements. More specifically, I walk up to my presentation practice area and stand silently for ten seconds to make eye contact with several of the imaginary people I'm presenting to, before I come out with a bang on my first words. I set my upper register right away, making it easy to tap the full spectrum of highs and lows across my talk. This practice gets me very used to starting strong, and I don't have to work at it much in the real thing.

Dynamic Drill #3: Tempo

Dynamism is as simple as talking fast, and then talking slowly.

Tempo has consistently proven itself as one of the most powerful dynamic builders we've seen.

I don't believe there is an ideal speaking pace, but I do recognize that anxiety pushes many people to rush their presentations. The speed itself wouldn't be a problem, except that they never deviate from it, so audiences get a high-speed flat line. If you can get a fast-talker to alternate between fast and slow, then suddenly their pace is dynamic. I tell people to *talk faster and slower*, leaving a space for the stress-induced speed and creating a dynamic range by adding in the other end of the spectrum. You're after an unpredictable pattern of switching between fast and slow to create dynamic highs and lows.

This dynamic works the exact same way as volume does, setting up a spectrum of change and resulting in huge bursts of authentic personality that emerge through it.

No particular place in your presentation needs to be fast or slow. In a real presentation, your speed should change whenever the spirit moves you. But the spirit isn't going to move you unless you practice letting it move you. So the repetitive practice of alternating fast, then slow, fast/slow, fast/slow, will hard-wire the likelihood in you, allowing you to break from monotony and respond to impulse.

It's not as much about the speed as it is the *change.*

I tend to slow down when I want to draw my audience's attention, but other speakers do the opposite, and for them speeding up seems to draw attention just as effectively. The *change* in speed signals to the audience that something different is coming, so their attention spikes with speed changes in either direction.

When you maintain tempo for an extended time, audience attention will gradually fade. Make a speed change, and you've pulled them back in and regained their attention.

A word bout slow.

Fast is easy to grasp. But talking slowly often requires some explanation. Slow is not like reducing the speed on the tape recorder and r-r-r-e-e-e-l-l-i-i-n-n-g-g words out in slow motion. Slow is accomplished by placing large gaps between words.

One of our clients who was facing a high-stakes sales pitch with lots of pressure needed some coaching. He is a fast talker and when he's under pressure, he goes crazy-fast. Because he's very smart and

has too much to say, he tends to present at a speed most listeners can't follow.

When addressing that challenge, we didn't tell him to talk slowly. We told him to "talk fast, *then* slowly." We pushed him to talk faster than he normally did, followed by talking w—a—y slower than he normally ever would by inserting gaps between words or phrases. After a while,

he developed a new normal with highs and lows in his tempo that addressed the fast-talking problem while giving him a place to be fast.

He imagined that he had a pocket full of "Grand Canyons," or big gaps to represent pauses and the mission to drop them randomly inside his sentences. A Grand Canyon-sized pause is pretty substantial and at first, he couldn't do it. He gave us only ditches and ravines so we had to stress that we wanted

Grand...

> *...Canyon...*

> > *...sized...*

> > > *...gaps.*

We needed something more like this:

"I need to practice (ditch) this simple process (ditch) so I will be able to talk (ditch) very (ditch) slowly (ravine), until (ravine) we can get (ravine) beyond proficiency (ditch) to actually master (Grand Canyon) this very (ditch) simple (ditch) practice."

After a few run-throughs, he was starting to get the hang of it. The eventual result was truly transformational. He seemed calmer and more together, and now his tempo gave the prospective client/audience time to process and understand his words.

He won the project.

Excluding emotion, tempo gives our clients the biggest bang for their buck. With minimal practice, they experience huge value from mastering this dynamic.

Dramatic pauses create more time to think.

You'll notice a powerful side benefit of changing your pace stemming from the addition of frequent moments of silence. Use the full range of dynamic pacing, including silent pauses. This will make it difficult for the audience to tell the difference between when you make a dramatic pause and a pause to find your place.

Show them that you intentionally pause for effect and they'll interpret any moment where you need to stop and think to be part of your dynamic style. In their eyes, you'll never lose your place again, and this will reduce your panic reflex while creating more processing time for both you and the audience.

Use pacing and pauses
to turn your awkward moments
into your dramatic style.

Talking slowly remedies the 'ums' and 'ahs.'

Heavily varied tempo also will put an end to the "ums" and "ahs." Fast and slow tempo, with dramatic silent pauses, fixes the problem at the source. This is a direct contrast to the unhelpful practice of "um counting," used by some presentation trainers. Focusing on *not* saying *um* tends to make it worse. It's like pointing out each individual stutter to a stutterer and hoping to bring an end to his problem.

A real solution requires that you grasp the real cause. Ums and ahs are caused by setting an unmaintainable pace—one that's too fast for your mind. The rate you can formulate thoughts, and convert them to words, is not a constant. Some sentences fall out of your mouth easily, and others require more time to articulate. Under the pressure of public speaking, you tend to start out a little too fast, and unwisely attempt to stick with the starting pace. Under the self-imposed expectation that it must continue without missing a beat, your brain will manufacture placeholder words (like ums or ahs) to fill any missing beats, while it finds the words to finish a sentence. It's a poor cover-up, but your brain doesn't think it has a choice *unless you give it one.*

Speaking with varied pace gives your mind the chance to process normally. Talking at a massively varied pace, from very fast all the way down to full stop, creates a totally different expectation. Your brain starts actively inserting silent pauses instead of ums, and your unconscious need to utter a place holder sound goes away.

Be sure to do a couple practice runs with a part of your presentation, focusing on very fast and very slow, with unbearably long silent pauses; put wherever (ravine long pause) the spirit (even longer Grand Canyon pause) moves you to do so. The longer the pause you practice, the more time you will have to breathe, strategize and course-correct on stage. And, pleasantly enough, the more opportunity your audience will have to process what you've already said, and anticipate what you're going to say next.

Give yourself the gift of silent pauses, and end the need for 'ums.'

Dynamic Drill #4: Gesture

Dynamism is as simple as talking with your hands, and occasionally dropping them to your sides.

Gesture is a booster of your dynamism. It transforms words into whole-body communication. A common question that comes with this is: "What do I do with my hands?"

You should do whatever you normally do with your hands when you talk. The problem is, you aren't normally paying attention to how you talk with your hands, so emulating something you're not aware of can be challenging.

Emotion is the default controller of gesturing, so it's a delicate thing to toy with. However, there are several reasons to spend some time with the dynamic of gesturing:

1. People have a very common, and quite obvious tendency to try to contain their hands when they're speaking. They are universally inclined to try to bind their hands, in front, in back or in pockets which runs counter to the instinct to freely express using hands. That conflict creates key rattling, wringing hands and twitchy fingers.

2. It's important to note *where* you're gesturing, and where you're directing your audience member's attention— hopefully to our face and not below the belt.

3. How you gesture affects your leadership presence. Based on what we've seen, about 90 percent of presenters have some room to improve in this area.

Practice pushing your gestures bigger than normal to train your hands to freely express themselves. Most people do the opposite and create nervous tics as they try unsuccessfully to hold themselves back. Perhaps this is motivated by a desire to look more formal, but more likely, hand-binding is an attempt to hide quivering hands. They tremble because of an overabundance of energy at a time when you're asking them to hold still. Gesturing is a simple solution to reducing the shakes, to give that energy somewhere to go.

Since gesture is a dynamic, it's another spectrum of highs and lows which tells us that sometimes you want to be gesturing, and other times you want to stop. Try alternating between gesturing and not gesturing during a rehearsal. Alternate sentence by sentence or at random. Sometimes your hands should be all over the place, abstractly helping you describe what you're saying. Other times your expression should drop away, leaving you in the gesture equivalent of a pause.

In a presentation, gesturing and not gesturing isn't a 50/50 balance. You should probably gesture most of the time and pause like punctuation in a paragraph. That way your gestures aren't a long run-on body language sentence.

Most people gesture just fine, but question it out of self-consciousness. Gesture is abstract, like a quasi-sign language that speaks to passion, energy and conviction without communicating anything specific, like verbal language does. So gesture the way you normally do and feel confident about it. The tricky part comes in how you pause.

When gestures pause.

Where do your hands go when they stop gesturing? Most likely, they go just above your waist, loosely clasped together. If you're lucky, this looks relaxed, like a cute little basket made of your arms and hands.

If you're overly stressed you may look like a *basket case*—fidgeting in nervous anticipation of getting back to your seat—or perhaps you'll bear a resemblance to an evil villain wringing his plotting hands..

If you don't basket your hands, you'll likely put them behind your back, like a soldier in at-ease position. But if you're sporting anything short of a Marine's confidence, you'll look more like someone in handcuffs.

If you don't basket or 'soldier up,' you'll probably use your pockets like holsters for your hands. You may do the one-gun hand-holster, freeing the other hand to wave around or you may do a two-gun hand holster, putting both hands in your pockets. This looks strangely restrictive and draws attention below the belt, especially if you start rattling your keys and coins.

The gender of gestures.

Having watched literally thousands of presenters, I've seen some very straightforward gender tendencies, but I have no idea what's behind them.

Nearly every woman I've ever seen present, defaults to the basketing gesture, putting her hands together at her waist. Many have told us that someone in a speech class told them to do that. Basketed hands is unquestionably acceptable. It's just not as powerful as it could be.

Lots of men basket too, but many men like the handcuffs resting pose, and a smaller percentage holster their hands in their pockets. I don't think I've ever seen a woman utilize the hand-holsters. I've never seen a woman key-rattler either. It might be that men's clothing almost always has actual pockets where women's skirts and slacks typically don't.

While there is some gender variance in the bad habits of gesture, the gesture guidelines we recommend at SagePresence have no bias. Gesture is about freeing your expressions from the cage, recognizing that you're likely holding the cage door closed with your hands.

What all hand-control strategies have in common.

Baskets, cuffs and holsters are *protective gestures*. They serve the same function as a podium—to create some false sense of security against a nonexistent danger, like a favorite blanket for a kid who's afraid of the dark. You can't hide when you're the presenter. And locking down your hands tells everyone that you're still struggling with that idea.

Most of us know that we shouldn't cross our arms when talking to an audience because it looks blocked off and insecure. Basketing is just a relaxed version of crossing our arms. Cuffing is a relaxed version of basketing. Pocketing raises a lot of questions, especially when you rattle stuff. Technically, all of these are accepted, but on some level, they communicate your fear. Why do that?

When you gesture, you look free and expressive.
When you let your arms hang at your sides, you look confident.

A better "What to do with my hands" strategy.

Presenting is an activity where you have a lot of extra energy. Letting your hands participate gives you a good place to put that energy. Practice setting them free—with occasional pauses—by putting your hands at your sides.

Gesturing looks free and normal, creating the sense of an intimate conversation. Hands at your sides looks very strong and unguarded, sending a signal of utter confidence—no need for self-protection. Doing both shows you as *naturally confident*, an unbeatable combination.

Check in with yourself here and there throughout your day, and build some awareness of how you normally let your hands talk alongside your words. The more used to checking in you are, the less you'll be thrown off when paying attention to it in practice.

Gesture up by your face most of the time,
and occasionally drop your hands to your sides as a pause.

"But I've been told my gestures are distracting!"

Here I tell you to gesture most of the time, when someone else has said that you gesture too much. Some people, usually men, have actually been told that their gestures are distracting. Perhaps it is because they are using only one gesture and repeating it frequently.

Normal hand-talk is varied. Repetitive gestures can be distracting. The classic culprits are the 'power-pyramid,' the 'counting gesture,' and the one or two-handed 'praying gesture.'

Most of the people who fall victim to the patterns of repetitive gesturing don't gesture that way normally. This is a presenting pattern, emerging as a response to the pressure of being in front of groups. If you have this repetitive problem, practice *changing* your gestures in rehearsal to introduce your brain to new and varied patterns.

Gesture practice—move outside the box, then stop altogether.
Practice using as many different gestures as possible. This will create a muscle memory of variety in your gestures. Use your hands in new ways and you'll expand your own expressive parameters.

Occasionally, like commas and periods in a sentence, practice dropping your hands to your sides and talk for a sentence while your hands essentially hang limp. After another sentence, bring your hands back up near your face and gesture again, stopping after a few sentences with another short pause.

If your hands are at your sides, you may feel your fingers starting to flinch. That's their way of saying, "Hey! I'm down here. Please release me. I've got some extra energy here, and I want to participate." If your fingers are twitching, or tugging at the seams of your pant legs, this means you need to gesture *more*. Let that flinch be your signal to bring your hands up, and set them free to say what they want.

Explore gesturing in a practice,
but forget about it in a real presentation.

Extra Credit: **The best start, hands down.**
Want to start with a bang? When you walk up to your audience at the start of your talk, leave your arms at your sides. This shows them right away that you are confident. Make silent eye connections with three or four people, and start talking when your eyes are on the fourth. Keep your hands loosely at your sides for another few sentences.

If you can show right out of the chute that you are secure, you will establish yourself in your audience's eyes as a confident presenter. When you suddenly surprise them with a gesture, they will see a speaker who is free and genuinely comfortable enough to express their feelings.

Dynamic Drill #5: Movement

Dynamism is as simple as walking while you talk, taking at least three steps, then stopping like a pillar.

I think of moving around the room the same way I think of moving the camera when I'm directing a movie. Cinematographers move because it changes the angle and refreshes the view, thereby keeping the audience's attention. Movies also increase intensity by moving in close, before relaxing out to a wide shot.

You can accomplish the same goals with a presentation audience by moving around. You walk to change their view. Walking while you talk gives them a 'traveling shot.' Backing up opens the stage like a wide shot, perhaps for broader concepts, and moving up to the audience is a lot like a close up, which is great for *über* important stuff.

"But the podium is already there!"

Half the conventions I speak at have a podium already in place for me to hide behind. I ask the organizers to move it or slide it out of the way. If there's room to leave it and still be able to move around, I might start behind it just to pull a surprise move and come out from it. To me, this is *leaving the cage* symbolism—I start out inside then fly out, never to return.

Early on, I try to find an audio/visual person to see if I can score a wireless mic so I don't need to take the podium microphone, or I check myself to see if the configuration allows enough cable for me to walk around. I strongly recommend doing this. Several times, I've undone black tape to free up more cable, or I've set the entire podium off the stage before anyone could stop me. "Oh, hey, I moved the podium off the stage. Do you want me to move it back when I'm done speaking?" They usually don't.

Only three times in ten years did I ultimately get stuck behind a podium. In those cases, mobility was notably hampered, so I relied on my volume, tempo and emotions to bring dynamism through my voice. I could still do eye-contact dynamically, and to a small degree, I could lean forward, back, or to the side, but mostly I relied on voice.

Activate your audience.

Moving makes the audience more active. They turn their heads, follow you with their eyes and sometimes even reposition their chairs for a good view. It may not be much, but it disrupts the possibility of an audience member parking his face in the palm of his hand to daydream or sleep.

A walk in the park.

A walk in the park is a great metaphor for walking during a presentation—just walk while you talk. The strolling conversation creates an experience of having room to breathe, and creates a three-dimensional experience, where standing behind a podium gives you a more limited, two-dimensional view. Go different directions, forward and backward and at angles. Try different speeds. It creates a sense of space, even when there isn't much room. I've seen speakers run up to their audiences, or slowly creep in and out. Some even move past the first row *into* the crowd at times, forcing people to turn around in their chairs to see them.

You can find a lot of ways to move on a stage, just like you find different ways to walk through a park. Some people jog, some stick to the trails, some prefer the grass and others jump the fence, hop on rocks, and climb the trees. Your personality will dictate how you use the floor, but everyone enjoys a conversation on the move with some fresh air to breathe.

Moving helps audiences organize content.

Moving and stopping creates a series of *journeys with a destination.* You are not going anywhere, but it feels like you are, just like in the movies where you feel you've been taken to infinity and beyond, even though you've never left your seat. Moving on stage—provided that you also stop sometimes—creates a similar sense of journey and destination.

As you find yourself wrapping up a topic, stop moving and finish the subject. Pause a moment, move on to the next subject, walking and talking as you go. Imagine that you're stepping out on another stroll. This can communicate the same thing to an audience as a chapter heading in a book or a title card in a movie. You're reinforcing the structure of your presentation, helping the audience to grasp your message with the way you walk around.

I've watched good speakers do this, surely unintentionally. Obviously something must happen that inspires the brain to take a step, so it's probably intuitive to move when topics shift. When we at SagePresence teach our clients to do this, we immediately see their presentations come alive.

Moving as content.

When I can, I take my movement-as-structure concept even further by associating certain concepts with specific areas of the floor. For example, whenever I'm teaching story structure, I establish the beginning way over to stage right (that's *left* to the audience). I do this by walking stage right when I say that part. Next, I'll run all the way over to stage

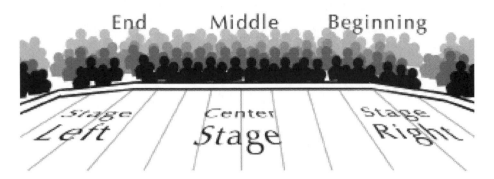

left (*right* to the audience) when talking about end. I talk about middle from center stage. Since my audiences read left to right, I am visually embodying beginning, middle and end as they would see it on a page.

Later on, when I demonstrate telling a story, all I have to do is stand stage right when I'm at the beginning, center stage during the middle and stage left at the end and the audience can visually plot my progression through the story, and anticipate where we are, based on where I am on the stage.

In that way, my strolls around the stage are actually part of the content, and movement allows me to reinforce without repeating.

As a speaker, I'm not afraid to go off on an improvisational tangent. I'll deviate from my plan if I think a story might help me connect the dots to an audience question, or if I think I have a useful elaboration that came to me in the moment. I often establish a specific area on the floor to stand in whenever I'm venturing off course. I call that my 'oh, by the way' place and relegate any asides to that spot. That way, the audience can see them coming because I move over to share from that space.

You can find or invent a lot of creative ways to use the floor. It's one more opportunity few people consider that can help you stand out and make your message stick.

Practicing movement.

Do at least one practice where you forget about getting anything else right and work exclusively on using the floor during that run. Moving well in rehearsals ensures capturing attention in the presentation. specifically practice getting closer to the audience at important moments.

Here are some valuable guidelines to keep in mind as you practice in front of empty chairs:

1. **Three-Steps Rule:** If you're going to move, MOVE—and that means a *three-step minimum*. If you take only one or two steps, that's either a nervous shuffle or the 'pee dance.' But if you take three good steps it will feel intentional and graceful. There's no upper limit. You can take 20 or even 50 steps, if you have a big enough stage—but at least three, which you can fit into even a very tiny space if that's all you have.

2. **Stop Rule:** Movement is great, but if you don't stop, you'll look like a caged animal. Take your three or 50 steps, talk while you walk, but then stop, giving the journey its destination. Stay put for a while. Maybe 30 seconds. Be a pillar. Then you can move again.

3. **Golfer Rule:** People stop in the craziest poses, particularly women—and men like me who wear cowboy boots. It's the shoes. They promote weight-shifting to rest on one foot, the basis of many a strange pose. Practice stopping squarely, with toes and heels of both feet on the floor, like a golfer on a putting green.

Dynamic Drill #6: Emotion

Dynamism is as simple as opening yourself up to feeling your words while you say them.

This book has extensively analyzed the power of emotions. You now realize your power to inspire others by feeling what you say, and you recognize the constructive uses for happy, sad and mad. You also discovered the driving, super-charged energy of the Happy/Mad Cocktail for when you really need a magnetic boost of influence.

Practice feeling your words. Control the chemistry of your presence through your connections with your audience. You have explored five powerful dynamics that can prime your body to express your authentic feelings.

Let go and trust your heart.

Emotion is something to practice. Don't wait for the real thing to find out how much heart you can put into something. If you can't let go in your own safe environment, how can you expect to feel anything under the heart-stopping pressure of the stage?

Ask yourself: *Can I open myself up to feeling my words as I say them?* Give yourself permission to feel, and make an activity out of emotional availability. Practice at least one section of your talk with an emphasis on feeling it.

Points to remember:

1. Emotions control body language far and above anything else.
2. Having worked on the other drills, your body is ready to express.
3. In emotion rehearsals, abandon exaggerated expressing. Just feel your feelings genuinely, and let your body express them naturally.
4. Appreciate, embrace and enjoy vulnerability. Give yourself permission to feel.
5.   Rehearse emotions in different locations so you don't limit your zone of comfort to just one place.

6. Save your performance for the show. Don't practice emotions on event day, unless you have at least a few hours before the event to rebuild your energy.

A final note about dynamics.

These dynamic guidelines have mostly been applied toward standard formal parts of your presentation. I sometimes break these rules in the *informal* parts of my presentation. I get really casual sometimes, when the moment calls for it, and when it seems more formal, I adjust accordingly. That way, casual or formal, I will be consistently viewed as professional.

The other venues: camera, meetings and conversations.

At SagePresence, we offer specific training to address the needs of unique venues. We've looked at six basic dynamics for public speaking, and in general they all relate pretty directly to all the other venues. However, there are some exceptions and some details that need to be pointed out for these other venues.

On-camera.

Imagine there is a master control, like a volume dial, for dynamism. The principles we looked at for public speaking are mostly identical here, but some of them need to dial down as you come off the stage and get in front of a camera because your audience is in the lens, intimately within your one-on-one space.

We work with some companies who present to a live audience, with a second group viewing them remotely via camera. In this instance, we recommend first making eye contact with two people in the room, and then making eye contact with the camera (which reaches all the remote viewers at once), then connecting with two more live audience members and returning to the camera again. This pattern works really well. Appreciating the camera with direct eye contact is specifically what creates a 'connected experience' to a viewer.

a. Eye contact is basically the same in that you're either making connections directly with the lens of the camera or with an interviewer or fellow on-camera talent. Appreciation practice with a camera lens can be very helpful—really see the lens, and actively appreciate it. Or, you can imagine someone else standing in place of the camera and you can appreciate them when you talk to the camera.

b. All the ideas about tempo are exactly the same for creating on-camera interest, but you have to scale your overall dynamism to fit the amount of camera time you have. If you're being interviewed for the news for example, you often only have a few minutes to make a couple key points. You won't have the freedom to use hundreds of Grand Canyon pauses. Sometimes you have to choose between a dynamic read with less content, or a content-rich, fast read. Performance-wise, I prefer changing pace (saying less rather than packing in too much information) for a dynamic read, if at all possible.

c. Volume, gestures and movement are still correct as principles, but they often have to be dialed down from stage level to conversational level. Talk to the audio tech in advance to test the limits of how loud and soft you can be.

    And check in with the camera operator to find out where the edges of the frame are so that you can make sure your gestures can be seen and aren't too big. Movement on-camera is not always possible. You're commonly going to be stationary when you're interviewed for the news or creating footage for the Internet. But if your stage presentation is being captured on video, the rules are the same.

d. Emotion works exactly the same way for camera as it does for public speaking. You want to feel it, and the more authentically you express emotion, the more effective you are on-camera. Video is essentially an attempt to emulate an actual conversation experience so you want to open up on video and emote like you would in an intimate conversation.

Meetings.

Our recommendations for meetings are very similar to public speaking guidelines, especially when you are standing and presenting an idea or an argument. If you're sitting and talking in a meeting, most everything is the same except dial it down to the level of intimacy or formality that the table discussion warrants.

a. Eye-contact, emotions and tempo are exactly the same. Look at people directly, with appreciation, for about a sentence. Feel your words and determine the best level for the circumstance. Fast and slow tempo creates dynamic speed, as it does on stage.

b. Your gestures will be reduced, naturally affected by the smaller amount of space you're in. When you're sitting at a table, I recommend resting your hands on the tabletop when they're not 'saying' anything, so that they're always available to communicate when they want to.

c. With volume, you're probably never going to get as loud as you might get when you're presenting in front of a room, but you still want to explore an upper and lower register to maximize your dynamism and keep their attention.

d.   Movement is different. If you're sitting at a chair, you can't exactly walk around. But you can lean forward to zoom in and intensify. You can lean back at more casual moments. I try to be dynamic in the chair and move in as close as possible at important times, and when I'm calling for action. A great way to physically remind yourself to stay dynamic is to sit on the edge of your seat, poised and ready to express at any time.

Conversations.

In conversation, all the basic principles of the dynamics of public speaking apply. Like on-camera, they are dialed down to the intimacy level of the conversation at hand.

a.   In a one-on-one conversation, you should spend a lot of time making eye contact with the other person. You can look away to think, or even talk to the ceiling or floor for short moments. However, the bulk of the dialogue should be spoken with laser eye contact.

Leaders make more eye contact than followers, so I try to model this in conversation. Remember that the difference between aggressive and warm eye contact is appreciation, so look into their eyes with this feeling, and you'll project leadership presence without being intimidating.

b.   Emotion in conversation simply needs to be felt, and expressed authentically.

c.   Volume, tempo and gestures should change dynamically, but they will automatically reduce from what we described in public speaking to align with the intimacy level of the conversation.

All in all, the six dynamics apply to any venue, with a few differences— mostly that the 'master volume' of expression increases as more people are in front of you. Conversation and on-camera are essentially the same. Public speaking is much bigger in expressive level, but only because we want to create the intimate conversation experience from much farther away—like we're talking with a person across the street.

Meetings are in the middle, typically about half-way between an intimate conversation and a presentation.

Practice the six dynamics, and if you get them down for public speaking, you'll be set for everything else because it's always easier to dial down than it is to dial up. Adapting for meetings and conversations will likely be automatic and intuitive.

The six dynamics in review

There are six basic things to shift you from just saying words to truly engaging and maintaining our audience's interest:

- Eye contact
- Volume
- Tempo
- Gesture
- Movement
- Emotion

The first—eye contact—brings you into the connection. The last—emotions—inspires your audience with feelings that go through that connection. In the middle, we gave you tools to expand your range of expression—volume, tempo, gesture and movement. Any one of these alone can increase audience attention. Practice them all and you will clearly and visibly improve in the eyes of anyone you talk to.

These practices increase your tolerance for vulnerability, and loosen your body for freer expression. They align mind, heart, and body while expanding your ability to express. Ultimately, you will befriend vulnerability and discover that feelings are your greatest resource. Instead of hiding from them, train your body to express them and you will have the capacity to inspire.

Remember that you must practice these dynamics when it's safe, and trust them to be present during the presentation. As you step up before your audience, ask yourself to be open to your emotions. Ignite the feeling process with a deep appreciation for each person in your audience. Engage them one at a time. Forget about the rest. You've rehearsed all the dynamics, so they will be there for you. You've done the drills. Now play ball.

Dynamism is capturing and recapturing audience attention with the simple practice of changing stuff.

Chapter 7

Beyond Make-or-Break Moments

LYN CASADY: Your life is like a river. If you're aiming for a goal that isn't destiny, you will always be swimming against the current.

Script from the movie
"The Men Who Stare at Goats"

You have arrived.

And where you have arrived is actually at the start of your *real* journey—the adventure for which you need winning presence. You are standing in the doorwayfrom the the place where your authenticity no longer needs to hide, and you are looking bravely out toward a world that awaits your influence. You have embraced your own vulnerability to claim ownership of your moment, to walk the world with no holding back. You understand that all expression comes with emotional risk, but you bring your own safety with you, knowing you have everything you need to master the role you were born to play.

You know how to:

- Be comfortable in your own skin
- Appreciate your fear so it fuels you

- Authentically connect with even the most challenging audiences
- Structure messages that lead people where they need to go
- Keep listeners on the edge of their seats
- Integrate connection, message and dynamism to present your best under pressure
- Use your emotions as your most powerful asset for influence

The unattainable is now attainable. You have the skills that deliver presence and inspire chemistry. What do you intend to do with them?

Begin Your Journey of Growth

Don't let what we've started here fade.

A Chicago company where I helped coach a sales presentation asked my team back to do a refresher about six months after our first visit. I was thrilled to learn that people were still using the common language we'd given them. People were story-structuring messages, making connections and carrying an entirely new level of dynamism into presentations. One man in particular, previously crippled with fear and doubt, had become a remarkable presenter on far less information than I've shared with you. He had incorporated the simple principles into his daily regimen.

On other occasions, I've returned to companies where I had shared the same knowledge, having watched people change before my eyes, only to find they'd reverted to old ways—and the refresher seemed more or less like starting from scratch.

You can evolve on your own, or you can do it with us through our coaching, seminars, books and products. But please, evolve. Do it however you can. The next steps are yours alone to take—steps of integration and practice.

Integrating Connection, Message, and Dynamism in Life

The principles you've explored in this book can be applied on a number of levels. I've been writing about them as "speaking and conversation skills," but they are also relevant to how you pilot your life and how you lead inside your world.

You can wield confident passion, communicate with care and concern for others, and also see the intersection of stories that define a path to helping others on your journey.

I've shared what Pete and I have used to help individuals face make-or-break moments. This applies as much to professional interactions and presentations as it does to intimate conversations.

Elegant forces are at work here. Connecting the dots between your speaking skills and your life will make the skills stick and help you relate more powerfully to anyone with whom you interact.

Don't just use these skills. *Become* them. They will serve as defining traits—qualities central to you, and that differentiate you. They'll serve every choice you make as you shape yourself and the world around you.

Use the core concepts to:

- Master your make-or-break moments
- Grasp the bigger picture of your own life and career
- Lead your world

The more you use them, the more you can use them.

The Make-Or-Break Moment—A Close Up Life Experience

The pressure of performance in the moment can cause you to zoom in to a close-up experience of your life. You need to make an impact on a particular audience *right now*. You have a specific result in mind, and any number of things can get in your way.

But now, even in the heat of the moment, under the stress and the pressure, you can turn things around with the simple solutions you've explored.

You can CONNECT with your audience to get your attention off yourself and project confidence and caring.

You can create CHEMISTRY by being open to your own emotions and those of others, and you can lead that chemistry by intentionally setting the tone of the interaction.

You can create MESSAGES that others care about, that are structured to lead them exactly where you want them to go.

And you can deliver your messages with DYNAMISM. By using the energy of your fear to change simple things, you can capture and retain the attention of your audience.

All of this adds up to mastering the moments that previously rattled you. On some level they caused you to hide, keeping you from seeing the forest for the trees in your way. Now beyond your own cage, there is nothing stopping you from flying higher to witness the breathtaking vista of the forest of your goals.

Designing Your Life and Career—Finding Your Medium Shot

Zooming out from the close up of make-or-break moments, you land on the *medium shot* of your life. You can pull away from the pressure of the moment to look at your bigger picture goals and desires and create a story for yourself to live within and follow.

At SagePresence we do this with a program called LifeScript for professionals, job hunters and people facing a crisis. LifeScript successfully demonstrates that having a story-based plan can help you define a road map, and troubleshoot the obstacles in your way by putting yourself in a story you want to live.

Story helps you identify and define a happy ending beyond whatever challenge you're facing. Story helps you set a goal you would like to achieve. You can discern a not-so-happy beginning situation you're currently in that contrasts with the happy ending you want. And you can produce an action plan in the middle that can take you from where you are now to where you want to be. LifeScripting gives you authorship on the journey that is your life.

This action plan *must* include talking with other people—presenting to them, selling to them, building relationships with them, leading them and inspiring them. So your LifeScript is going to be full of make-or-break moments to which you can bring the skills of CONNECTION, CHEMISTRY, COMPELLING MESSAGES and DYNAMISM.

Leading Your World—Your Magnificent Wide Shot

Zooming out even farther, you will find a wide-shot that goes beyond your life to encompass the world around you and define how you will leave it for those who follow. You can use the skills you've learned in this book to make a difference beyond yourself and your life to create the change out in the world that you want to see.

You can apply the principles of story to identify a main character of a population you're dedicated to helping. Distinguish their not-so-happy beginning situation so it will resonate with them. Choose a happy ending that will inspire them. And identify an action plan that will take them from the not-so-happy beginning now to their future happy ending.

Then, you can enlist others to help. Use the skills of CONNECTION, CHEMISTRY, MESSAGES and DYNAMISM to engage them in a cause that inspires them to take action and make a difference.

Mastering The Role

Let's review all that you now know, capturing the depth of this content in only a few short sentences. SagePresence methodology is based on three core principles designed to leverage skills you already have.

Connection, Message and *Dynamism* are all you need in order to have confident presence and influence. This new presence will help you face a marathon of make-or-break moments that await you as you move down the road toward your goals. Without these skills you have to *walk*. Use the skills, and you get to *drive*. Become the skills, and you will *fly*.

1. Pursue appreciative *CONNECTIONS* with every opportunity for interaction.
2. Structure compelling *MESSAGES* that guide people from where they are to where they'd rather be.
3. Embody *DYNAMISM* by embracing irresistible change and pursuing highs and lows inside of everything you say.

These three concepts will create the experience of successful one-on-one conversation or speech everywhere you present yourself or your ideas.

Distilled further, you can land on just three words that will unlock *everything* contained in this book. It's the three-word operator's manual for the chemistry set of presence: APPRECIATION, STORY, CHANGE.

These are all you need to master presence when you present, network, sell, negotiate, interview and lead.

Believe In Yourself, and Claim the Leading Role In Your Life

I've now given you everything that Pete Machalek and I have devoted well over a decade to learn, test, compile and share.

With this gift comes an affirmation—that *I believe in you.*

With this affirmation also comes a burden. I expect you to succeed *and* to help others along the way. I expect everything you can deliver, and you need not report to anyone but yourself.

Give yourself permission and there will be:

- No one to fear—because you are the chemist responsible for the interactions that shape the world around you
- No one to let you in—since you hold the door that invites others in
- No one to decide what life you could lead
- Unlimited change to keep your experience fresh and exciting

Connect to the people around you, and lead them with your unbridled **APPRECIATION**. Bask in the effect of the chemistry between you and them. Your presence will mix with theirs to synthesize an experience as unique and individual as a snowflake.

Live both inside and outside of the **STORY** you craft for yourself. Within it, you experience life. Outside of it, you become the author. But it is just a story—it's still not you. If you perceive it, it can't be you. It's an adventure *for* you that you have created and chosen from which you can choose another at any time. Story is a context in which to place yourself and it's a context to explain everything else around you.

Be both the author and the title role in the *story of you* and recognize how your story intertwines with the stories of others. As you look at the larger tale of those around you, recognize that you can be a hero in their middle, helping them move from not-so-happy beginnings to happier endings.

CHANGE comes regardless of anything you do. And this is as it should be, because only a changing life inspires interest. Those who embrace change enjoy boundless passion and endless possibility, basking in the energy they create through the chemistry of presence.

Embrace the vulnerability,
and share yourself fully.
Then you shall stand
in your own light...the light of
Winning Presence.

Your Evolution Beyond this Book

> PROT: For your information, all beings have the capacity to cure themselves.
>
> *Script from the movie "K-PAX"*

You are at a crucial point in your development right now. You've absorbed a tremendous amount of information that is only going to represent potential value until you put it into action.

You've learned about what to do and how to practice in general. Now let me offer a single first action to take. This will solidify your commitment to apply your knowledge and realize tangible value for yourself.

It's a simple one: Sign up to receive the SagePresence blog at **SagePresence.com**.

Use this reference tool and share it with others you care about. It will provide you with free tips and reminders to get and stay in action and it is a place to reach out and communicate with others, ask questions and provide input. It will also give you access and special discounts for supportive materials we'll make available to you, including:

- Products that focus on the challenges of leadership, selling, public speaking, networking and negotiating
- Modules that address the needs of specific audiences, including professional women and people around the globe who want to influence American audiences

- Private coaching that provides a customized experience of elevating your presence and moving your career forward with velocity
- National workshops providing the opportunity to build your skills
- The possibility of becoming a Sage yourself, and joining our growing team of SagePresence trainers

Even more, your subscription to our blog will transform your potential into fully realized results. And your participation in the blog is going to give us the opportunity to hear from you directly and keep up to date on your development.

What Dean Hyers and SagePresence Can Do For You and Your Organization

> LUCIUS: I don't know what will happen. Only what needs to be done.
>
> *Script from the movie "The Village"*

Dean Hyers is an accomplished filmmaker, entrepreneur and international speaker with a committed passion for defending vulnerability. He splits his time between film projects, speaking and consulting. Schedule a keynote at **DeanHyers.com**.

Dean's company, SagePresence, helps business professionals move forward in their careers by giving them the tools they need to build professional relationships, present their core values and win over key audiences while networking, selling and interviewing.

SagePresence also elevates organizations on a number of levels:

- Helping executives present and lead with presence
- Guiding sales teams to win under pressure
- Leading team members to become active business-building ambassadors for the organization throughout its target markets
- Training staff to transform customer services challenges into business-building opportunities

- Coaching staff members to communicate internally with greater influence and effectiveness.

More information about programs, services and in-house products are available at **SagePresence.com.**

Acknowledgements

CLARENCE THE ANGEL: No man is a
failure who has friends.
Script from the movie
"It's a Wonderful Life"

The wings of SagePresence have strengthened over the years due to so many who have felt the power of our message and supported our evolution. We are grateful to these ambassadors and have appreciated a universe of support that has come from kind hearts interested in change for themselves and in others around them.

This book, our curriculum, the company SagePresence and a decade of making a difference are the result of my equal collaboration with Pete Machalek.

I thank filmmaker Rob Nilsson who generously shared his approach to authentic screen performance based on his improvisational filmmaker idol, John Cassavetes. He helped us start our acting workshop, which was our training ground for performance, and the first row of sturdy blocks in the SagePresence foundation.

My wife Kim, who is my truest and best friend, along with my boys Ethan and Aaron, have encouraged and supported me through this meandering trek now known as SagePresence. Their belief in me was the energy that kept me on track, following my compass northward through the fog to eventually reach a summit—planned to be the first of many.

A number of early adopters of our approach went out on a limb to support us when our knees were still weak. Renowned screenwriting guru Hafed Bouassida gave our workshop its first home at the Minneapolis Community & Technical College (MCTC). Cindy Schroeder (author of *A Hunt For Justice*) was a covert agent with the out-of-the-box idea to give filmmakers a crack at teaching acting to government undercover agents. This was a giant, sexy leap on our work history, giving us our marketing story and the courage to throw ourselves at what scared us.

John Stout of Fredrikson & Byron, P.A. has been a pillar in my ever-changing world, playing a role in every business venture I've had. John, along with Don Thomas, John Strachota and Brian Buchholz of BWBR Architects, gave SagePresence a footing in its most delicate years.

In 2003, psychologist Jennifer Gori collaborated with us on LifeScript, our 'narrative therapy' approach to overcoming roadblocks and designing lives and careers with the power of story. It was Jen who first put SagePresence before audiences of clinical psychologists, bringing validation to our methods.

Meanwhile, Cheryl Alexander was the first Executive Coach to collaborate with SagePresence. Cheryl paved inroads for us to teach at major business schools, and she connected the dots for us between our skills and leadership, particularly with professional women.

Endless thanks to Lauri Flaquer of Saltar Solutions, our business coach and brand designer since 2005. Lauri has been holding our hands every step of the way since we met, and she is instrumental today in evolving our vision and our success.

We want to thank Bill True, a screenwriter who thinks structure first, and words second. His insights helped us hone our grasp of the story structure that our clients rely on, and we enjoyed his co-presenting with SagePresence from 2007 to 2009, before he returned to Hollywood.

Mike Koenigs, founder of TrafficGeyser and my former business partner at Digital Café, was instrumental in our Internet marketing strategy, and he connected me to international speaking opportunities in

Mexico and Australia, which led to engagements in the United Kingdom. I am an international speaker because of Mike.

Helene Woods and the Minnesota Workforce Center helped us tap new audiences in dislocated worker programs. Stephen Bennett of Gustavus Adolphus College helped us reach placement programs for graduating students.

A very special thanks to Stephanie Menning and Jean Nitchals, who helped us build our national track record as speakers to professional women's associations. Stephanie founded the Energetic Women (part of the Midwest Energy Association). Jean helped position us with WOLF (originally Best Buy's Women's Leadership Forum), and later within the Network Buzz, a women's networking association. Their independent efforts placed SagePresence in six different states nationally with a strong local history with professional women.

Many hands have touched and many eyes have seen this writing as it was becoming a book. A massive contributor was my editor, Connie Anderson of Words and Deeds, Inc. Her contributions resemble those of my film editor Lee Percy, on my movie "Bill's Gun Shop." Both made what I had to say so much more by taking a tremendous amount out of it, streamlining, re-ordering and nurturing words and thoughts out of my long-winded expressions, honing in on what I was really trying to say. Also touching this work was Pete Machalek, Lauri Flaquer and editor Mary L. Holden, all of whom elevated the work I did to a higher level, getting me closer to what I'd hoped to accomplish, and keeping me truer to myself.

I also wish to thank Erl Morrell-Stinson, who is to my mind what Lauri Flaquer is to my business—an amazing coach who got me in touch with, thereby protecting, my truest cause. In this same vein of guidance, Tara Broughten reconnected me to spirit, insightfully forecasting an idea that I would become a writer, standing in my own light, and sharing my unique truths. The mentorship circle also includes Carry Metkowski, who brings insight and a plan, connecting our little ideas, to a grander, more powerful world.

I want to thank Jim Pagliarini, president of PBS affiliate Twin Cities Public Television, for helping me prove our techniques in the television studio. A special thanks to Robert Dempsey who unveiled to us the power of the Internet. Thanks also to Nick Tasler, author, speaker and peer who trusted me to coach and direct him even though he was farther down the path than I.

I want to thank my brother Jon Hyers, for the years of independent filmmaking together, which was an endless childhood that gave purpose to my teens and paved the way for my inner child to live a creative adulthood. Thanks and admiration to my sister Lauri Hyers, who boldly models protecting vulnerability in the world, a similar mission we take on in our own ways.

My final round of thanks includes my mother, Gerry Hyers, who showed me the melody of harmony, and whose genetics and nurturing gave me the night vision of emotional sensitivity, which later became my truest intelligence. And to my father, Conrad Hyers, who will always be my model for presenting and teaching. Thank you, Dad. Whenever I find my groove, I can feel your expressions inside my own face.

I'll end with a thanks to the late Peter Kuchera, who was a filmmaker friend from my twenties whom I never got to thank for one particularly inspirational statement. This has kept me going through every project and venture I've accomplished since the early nineties:

"Dean. Just do it. Any way you can."

About the Author

Dean Hyers believes he can help anyone be confident, dynamic and influential under pressure. Whether directing films, training U.S. and Canadian undercover agents to be believable or coaching sales teams to win multi-million dollar business pitches, he uses techniques from the movie set to direct professionals beyond their fears.

In 2001, Dean co-founded SagePresence, a company set up to help clients master professional roles with excitement and motivation and win over even their most challenging audiences. To date, SagePresence has helped innumerable individuals move forward in their careers and client companies win over 2 billion dollars in new business.

Prior to directing "Bill's Gun Shop" (an independent full-length feature, distributed by Warner Bros.), Dean co-founded Digital Café, a pioneer in the interactive media arena. Dean's company put the first CD-ROM in *Rolling Stone Magazine,* the first computer game in a cereal box, and marketed movies including "Godzilla," "Die Hard III," and "Jumanji," before its acquisition by advertising giant Campbell Mithun.

An engaging and charismatic speaker, Dean has entertained and informed audiences throughout the United States and in far-away places including Mexico, England, Ireland and Australia.